Advance Praise for BEHIND THE MASK

Kate's writing always connects with readers. She picks important and interesting subjects and writes about them in a way that people can identify with. Her writing style is accessible and compelling, and her honesty about whatever she's personally going through at that moment—or commenting about—really resonates. **—Lincoln Anderson, editor and publisher, *The Village Sun* (former editor, *The Villager*)**

A compelling memoir of the covid pandemic lockdown and its impact on one woman's life. Kate Walter—a longtime resident of the iconic Westbeth Artists community—shares the loneliness and sorrow of being isolated from family, friends, and activities. As she examines lessons learned throughout the ordeal, she rediscovers hope in often surprising ways. Each vignette is rich with engaging personal and contextual detail —from reflecting on her late mother's resilience to celebrating the presidential election outside the Stonewall Inn to mourning the tragic fire at her beloved Middle Collegiate Church to finally getting the vaccine. Beautifully written, this is a warmly insightful read with universal appeal. **—Carol J. Binkowski, author, *Opening Carnegie Hall: The Creation and First Performances of America's Premier Concert Stage***

Covid struck us in two dimensions, the public and the private. Kate Walter's chronicle of the plague year in Manhattan, from the ambulance sirens of one March to the vaccine hopes of another, illuminates both dimensions. It's a season-by-season journey narrative of one woman's progress through a city stunned yet bravely resilient and through the personal challenges faced by everyone who, like Walter, treasures the daily encounters that define urban living and the cosmopolitan spirit. These essays are vignettes of fear and loss, and, finally, of hope and determination. If we wonder how New York, and the rest of us, got through a terrible year, *Behind the Mask* just may have the answer. **—Bill Scheller, author, *America: A History in Art and In All Directions: Thirty Years of Travel***

BEHIND THE
MASK

KATE WALTER

Kate Walter

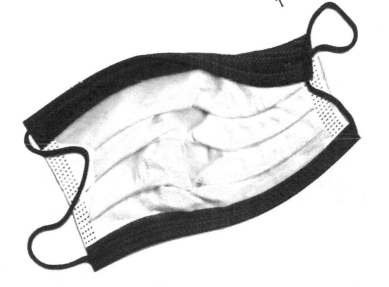

Living Alone in the Epicenter

Heliotrope Books

New York

Heliotrope Books LLC
heliotropebooks@gmail.com

ISBN 978-1-942762-81-2

Cover photograph by Kate Walter
Designed and typeset by Naomi Rosenblatt
Interior photographs courtesy of Kate Walter (pages 12, 29, 33, 34, 40, 44, 51, 60, 68, 95, 98, 110 129, 135, and front cover) and Naomi Rosenblatt (pages 16, 21, 47, 61, 126)

This book is dedicated to all my fellow
Americans who died from the coronavirus.
May they rest in peace.

Other books by Kate Walter:

Looking for a Kiss:
A Chronicle of Downtown Heartbreak and Healing

Table of Contents

Part One: Living Alone in the Epicenter

Preface 9

Westbeth Feels like a Ghost Town 13

Stayin' Alive 17

The Kindness of Strangers 22

Melting Down in Lockdown 25

Gay Pride in Isolation 30

Escaping to the Beach 35

Coming Out Again 41

Return from Trump Land 45

The Day Biden Won 48

The Pandemic Changed Me 52

My Pandemic Dreams 55

My Beloved Church Burns Down 58

Rita Houston 62

Home Alone for Christmas 64

The Old Party 66

Brief Encounters of the Pandemic Kind 69

Scheduling the Vaccine on my Birthday 73

Revising my Pandemic Routines 76

Hitting the Wall 78

Getting the Vaccine 80

The Second Time Around 83

Rooting for Hudson Street 86

On the Verge of Reentry 90

My Life Needs a Refresh Button 96

Getting Back Out There 99

I Know I've Been Changed 105

Postscript 111

Writing Prompts 113

Part Two: Life Before the Pandemic

Cleaning Out a Century of Family Life 119

Saving the Memory of Old New York 123

Signing a Legacy 127

Woodstock: My Queer Love Story 130

Acknowledgments and Credits 136

Preface

When I started writing about the pandemic in the spring of 2020, hundreds of people were dying every day in New York State. My hometown, New York City, was the epicenter of our country. It was hard to sleep as sirens wailed throughout the night. Ambulances rushed up the West Side Highway (which is on my corner), taking Covid patients to hospitals.

When I wrapped up this book in June 2021, the death rate in New York State had dropped to less than ten people every day. I read the emails from Governor Cuomo religiously during the pandemic. His emails documented the infection rate, how many people were hospitalized, how many people were intubated, how many people had died. The messages went from grim to hopeful.

In June 2021, I ran into a neighbor who works as a nurse in an emergency room. I asked how he was doing because I knew he'd gone through a rough time. He brightened up and told me they recently had a day when not one person came into his emergency room with Covid. Not one. New York City had turned a corner.

This memoir, *Behind the Mask*, is my personal story, my opinions and observations, my emotional reactions from my point of view as a journalist who lived through the pandemic in Manhattan. I thought I had seen a lot during my 45 years as a resident of lower Manhattan. (I witnessed 9/11 and the towers burning and falling. I lived through Superstorm Sandy, when the Hudson River rushed up my block and flooded the basement of my building, causing extensive damage.) But nothing like this had happened before. I felt it was important to document this extraordinary time period.

As New York reopened and the city started to return to normal, I was relieved but I also worried that people would forget what we had gone through and put the pandemic behind them. I'm happy to move on and enjoy everyday life again, but I never want to forget.

PART ONE:
Living Alone in the Epicenter

Westbeth Artists Housing, New York City, 2018

Westbeth Feels Like a Ghost Town: My Life Shut Down

MARCH 2020

The community room is closed. The gallery is dark. The spring flea market has been postponed. The community room and the gallery are the heart and soul of Westbeth Artists Housing. Everyone looks forward to shopping at the busy flea market in the basement.

The main lobby, normally bustling with activity and conversation, feels like a morgue. Management recently issued a memo that residents should only use the lobby for essential activities—no hanging out. I really feel bad for the seniors with mobility issues who use the lobby as a place to sit on a bench and socialize. Thankfully, it will get warm soon, and they will be able to go outside into the courtyard. Westbeth is a NORC, a naturally occurring retirement community, with many senior citizens in their 70s and 80s.

Whenever I go to the lobby to pick up my mail, I pass what my neighbor calls "the death board," where people post a photograph or a notice of a resident who just died. Some are expected. Some are shocking. Two years ago, a friend my age, a brilliant percussionist, had a heart attack while walking in the park. I worry about how Covid will impact Westbeth.

It's hard to believe that only two weeks ago, I gave a reading with three other writers in the community room. Over 50 people attended. I read the first chapter of a novel in progress, and everyone told me they liked it and wanted to know what would happen next. We mingled and chatted and drank champagne. The feedback was super encouraging. Just what I needed. It was the kind of interaction that makes Westbeth a great place for artists to live.

I've been a resident here since 1997. One of the best things about this complex is all the free and inexpensive activities that take place in the community room—classes, readings, concerts, puppet shows for the kids, under the auspices of the Westbeth Artists Residents Council. I often write in my gratitude journal, "I'm grateful to live in Westbeth."

Everything is now on hiatus. I loved the chair yoga class on Monday taught by the gifted Jennifer Gibson, who trained at Integral Yoga Institute. It really helped me cure my sciatica.

I totally looked forward to The Sing Time Sessions every Friday, taught by the talented jazz singer and Westbeth resident Eve Zanni. I've been a member of the "Bliss Singers" for over two years and made friends from inside and outside the building.

At our last meeting on March 13, we sat apart from each other but sang our hearts out. Eve assured us she'd send us music videos so we could practice our repertoire at home. Isaac Raz, our amazing pianist, dazzled us with his solos on "Swing, Swing, Swing." We ended the session with a heartfelt "We Shall Overcome."

I was almost crying when I said goodbye to my classmates, with the now-typical farewell, "Stay safe."

As I left the community room, I thought of that famous short story by Alphonse Daudet, "The Last Class." It's a tearjerker that made a big impression on me when I first read it in college in a world lit class (especially since I have Alsatian ancestry). It's about the last class taught in French after the Germans took over the region called Alsace-Lorraine. Now the virus was taking over my classes.

Losing all these activities is a major blow for someone like me who is single and lives alone. I'm a very outgoing, social person who really likes interacting with people. Adding to my social isolation, my church, Middle Collegiate, has stopped in-person worship and is going virtual.

When I last went to church, I wondered how we would "pass the peace" to our neighbors. Instead of shaking hands, we bumped elbows or put our hands in the prayer position and nodded to our neighbors. That was Sunday, March 8. Then I got a message that services would be streamed, and the following Sunday, I watched from home.

This current situation at Westbeth is very different than other disasters we weathered together. Along with my neighbors, we survived 9/11, watching the horror from our rooftop. We survived Superstorm Sandy, which flooded our basement and knocked out electricity. We carried food and water up the stairs. But those disasters brought us together as we helped our neighbors. The virus forces us apart.

But one thing is similar—the calmness and professionalism of our hard-working staff at Westbeth are reassuring. I so appreciate my neighbors being really friendly and saying, "Hi, Kate. How are you doing?"

Of course, there is so much uncertainty. No one knows if things will get better or worse with the virus. No one knows for sure if and when things will resume. The key word seems to be "postponed," not "canceled."

My singing class is supposed to resume later this spring. I can't wait and marked the date on my calendar.

I'm usually happy when it's spring, but this year, I'm feeling depressed and lonely. I know things could be worse. Other than being over 70, I'm not in any of the high-risk groups for the virus. I can still enjoy walking outside and going to the Greenmarket. And soon, I will plant my garden outside on Bethune Street. That will cheer me up.

I'm trying to look on the bright side of everything being canceled—being stuck in my apartment gives me time to finish my novel. I have no excuses now.

If I manage to survive this virus without getting sick, I will still suffer from anxiety, boredom, and social isolation. I already miss getting hugs from my friends. I miss the interaction of being with people. I know that things could be worse. I have a nice sunny apartment with food, wine, books, music. But I'm lonely.

I'm a member of the Whitney Museum and visited on March 10. I planned to meet a friend there a few days later, but now it's closed. I went to my writing group last week, but we are shifting to meeting online. The Strand Bookstore notified me I was getting a refund for two canceled readings. The New York Public Library (my second home) is closed. Restaurants and bars are also shutting down.

My life was going well until a few weeks ago. I'm happily retired from college teaching. Now I'm extra grateful I left because I never wanted to teach online. I'm a people-oriented person who liked interacting in a classroom. I love being out and about. Now I'm stuck.

All of this is depressing. I feel like I need an extra therapy session. But the virus has helped me to put things in perspective, especially my minor health issues. Things I worried about a few weeks ago seem relatively minor, like a funky crown that needs to be repaired or the sciatica that responded to acupuncture and yoga. Should I bother sticking to my blood pressure and cholesterol-reducing diet? Why deprive myself of things I love, like eggs and cheese and potato chips? I need comfort food.

Of course, I'm being careful, washing my hands like crazy, not hitting the elevator buttons with my fingertips (I use my knuckles), not touching door handles (I use my elbows). But there are so many things that we touch. I freaked out in the supermarket when I tapped the button on the credit card machine to hit enter. I now wear plastic gloves when I go to the store.

I'm grateful to be a healthy older person who walks two to three miles a day. At least walking in Hudson River Park has not been canceled.

NYC graffiti, 2020

Stayin' Alive

APRIL 2020

My social life has been canceled, and I just want to survive. My last normal day was March 12. I took the bus from the West Village to the East Village and met a friend in our usual lunch spot, the B&H Dairy restaurant. I had already texted her: no hugging. She ordered two blueberry blintzes and an egg cream. I ordered the Thursday special: four potato pierogis and a cup of vegetable soup.

We always discussed reading. I gave her a list of three books that I had really enjoyed recently: *The Dutch House* by Ann Patchett, *The Resisters* by Gish Jen, and *The World That We Knew* by Alice Hoffman.

After lunch, we lingered on Second Avenue in front of the Ottendorfer Library. My friend planned to go inside and ask the librarian to reserve them. She is a technophobe who does not know how to use a computer. I really went off on her, calling her a dinosaur.

I later texted an apology, blaming my outburst on anxiety over the virus. She said it was okay. She does not have email, and she is not on social media. I told her this was limiting.

My friend's son ordered her a Kindle. I wondered how she would download the books since she doesn't have an Amazon account. Maybe he can do that for her. I've always had this pet peeve about baby boomers who are technologically incompetent. Now it's not just making us look old; it's adding to the isolation. She felt that getting a Kindle was a step toward progress. One step at a time.

Looking back, that conversation seems prescient. Since I'm staying inside, my entire life is interacting on Facebook, attending classes and workshops that are streamed or Zoomed. Before last month, I had never attended a Zoom meeting.

I attended my church service (streamed). I took two qi gong

classes with teachers I know. One was live on Facebook, broadcast from my neighbors in Westbeth. The other one (on Zoom) was taught by Nadiya Nottingham, a priestess of Bridget who practices Celtic shamanism. Born in Ireland, she is funny and poetic and has a lovely brogue.

I signed up for an ongoing Zoom workshop with Mary Ellen O'Brien, a spiritual teacher I'd met at Omega. She spoke about trying to avoid getting swept into "the fear tornado." I really like that expression. My life was moving onto Zoom. The sessions included meditation and channeling. We were setting energy boundaries, listening to our inner guidance.

I was still in denial on March 12. I didn't even wear plastic gloves when I went outside, although I made a point not to touch the bus door with my fingertips and then to sanitize them. That was the last time I rode the bus before the lockdown.

The day it really hit me was Sunday, March 15, when I was asked to attend an emergency planning meeting in the Westbeth community room. The president of our Board of Directors said he was in close touch with Governor Cuomo and that Cuomo was going to close down the city and there would be hospitals in places like the Javits Center.

"This is war," someone said.

The main purpose of the meeting was to organize team captains for each floor to be links between the Board of Directors and the Residents Council. Westbeth has many vulnerable residents, including people with Alzheimer's and full-time home attendants. I signed up to be a floor captain. We would get groceries or meds for anyone who needed help and print out memos for residents without email.

I left the meeting scared, knowing this was going to be bad. I contemplated leaving the city. I have a small bungalow on the Jersey Shore and was tempted to flee. I'm not wealthy at all. I inherited this cozy cottage when my mother died, and I co-own it with two siblings. The beach house is still closed for the winter, although it's not a big deal to turn the utilities back on. But it's actually smaller than my one-bedroom apartment, and I don't have a car. Even under normal circumstances, there's nothing to do on that island in the off-season. I'd be bored out of my mind, so I decided to stay home in Westbeth with my books and instruments and good Wi-Fi and supportive neighbors.

Luckily, I love my apartment since it appears I will be stuck inside for a while. I live in a 600-square-foot loft, all open space, with high ceilings and great light. From my windows on the eighth floor, that face north, I have a partial view of the Empire State Building. The glow reassures me at night, a beacon of stability in this uncertain time.

The next time the reality slammed me was on March 31. That's when I found out that Pete, a good friend of mine in New Jersey, had Covid and was home very sick. I was checking on him because he has a vulnerable job and can't work remotely. We were texting, and I said, "Do you want me to call?" and he said, "No, I can't talk. I'm coughing so much."

He later texted back his test results: positive.

Only a few weeks ago, Pete and I were making plans for the Fourth of July holiday in Ocean Grove, which we've been doing for years. I texted him that I put him on the prayer list of my church and my yoga center. He's a single gay man, very close to his sister. But she's probably quarantined now. A mutual friend has volunteered to go to the store, leave stuff on his porch. I have known Pete since the '70s. I am so worried.

I'm also talking on the phone more. I spoke with my first cousin Eileen, a psychologist at a nursing home. Eileen told me to stay strong and stay calm and try to control the things I can control. She described the situation at the nursing home: residents are trapped inside their rooms. All activities have been canceled, and no more group dining.

She checks in on her clients from the hallway. A resident told her she is lucky she can go home. Every day, as she enters the workplace, someone takes her temperature.

I also have weekly conversations with Jennifer, one of my best friends from high school. We had lost touch over the years, but we reconnected at our 50th reunion a few years ago. I was amazed she'd lost her New Jersey accent. Not even a trace. Talking to Jennifer reminded me of when we were teenagers, chatting on the phone every night, my mother yelling at me to hang up because she was expecting a phone call from my aunt.

She lives in Phoenix and works as a professor of sociology at Arizona State University. She always taught online, so her professional life hasn't changed much. Jennifer is divorced, a mother to three adult children, including a gay son, who all live on the East Coast. She lives alone and can't see her children or grandchildren because of the pandemic.

On a good day, I go for a solitary walk and maybe see a neighbor, and we talk from six feet away. It was actually comical when I was shouting to this woman who I think is hard of hearing. Then again, maybe my voice was just garbled because I was talking through a face mask. I finally started wearing one even though I'm not immunocompromised.

At Westbeth, it is now one person at a time in the elevator (unless you are family), and we were asked to only check our mail twice a week in order to maintain social distancing in our mailroom (unless we are expecting an urgent piece of mail).

Before this pandemic hit, Westbeth Artists Housing was gearing up to celebrate our 50th anniversary. (The first tenants arrived in May 1970.) My choral group was working on versions of songs arranged by Gil Evans, who lived here.

Now residents are staying in touch through our website. I love this great series on it called "Westbeth Chronicles." This project was planned months ago, but now it's more meaningful. Residents were invited to contribute a short memory to it.

I'm grateful to the hard-working staff at Westbeth, who are working diligently to sanitize everything, swabbing the elevator buttons with alcohol. The smell is oddly reassuring. And they are doing a great job checking in the many packages that are filling up our lobby. They will get the biggest tip ever at the holidays.

I appreciate the workers in the grocery stores who travel here on the empty subway to ring up my groceries and stock the shelves.

I have incredible admiration for all the doctors and nurses working on the front lines in the hospitals. Compared to their sacrifices, staying home alone is nothing.

Music is another thing getting me through. I'm listening to chant music (kirtan) and chanting along. Not only is it relaxing, but I'm sending out healing vibes into the universe.

I'm a big fan and member of WFUV 90.7. I always tune into DJ Rita Houston's show "The Whole Wide World" on Friday nights, but now this program feels life-sustaining. I cried when Rita played Van Morrison's "Till We Get the Healing Done." I was dancing around to the Bee Gees' "Stayin' Alive." This is my new mantra.

Covid 19 Memorial at Tompkins Square Park, New York City, April 2020

The Kindness of Strangers

APRIL 2020

Talk about the kindness of strangers. On Saturday, April 11, I posted on the bulletin board app Nextdoor that I was looking to buy computer paper locally. Of course, I can order from Amazon, but delivery takes a while. Staples is a long walk, and I stopped taking the bus.

This woman answered that she had paper in her apartment, and she'd be happy to give it to me. I walked over to a building on Bleecker Street, and this neighbor I'd never met before came downstairs and dropped two reams of high-quality printer paper into my tote bag. I felt so grateful. I was down to my last ten sheets of paper. Now I had a thousand. She said she was glad it would go to good use.

The next day, Sunday, April 12, I left my apartment in Westbeth and walked to D'Ag's, the pricey supermarket on the corner, to buy the *New York Times*. The masked cashier was really friendly. She wished me a happy Easter. I wished her the same, thanked her, and left.

Last year, I took the bus across town to the East Village for an incredible service at Middle Collegiate Church on Second Avenue. The altar was filled with lilies. The pews were packed, everyone clapping and swaying as the choirs blasted out a rocking version of the Hallelujah chorus from Handel's "Messiah."

This year, I watched the service live-streamed. The digital team did a great job, pulling up music from the archive and creating new music by patching in singers and organists performing in their apartments. We wished each other a happy Easter in the chat box. Reverend Dr. Jacqui Lewis, the senior minister, read the gospel and preached about "the time between the now and the not yet."

Normally, I returned from church and took the subway to Port Authority, where I got the bus to Wayne, New Jersey. Then, someone from
my family picked me up. This was the first time in my life I would not
share Easter dinner with my large extended Catholic family.

My sister has nine grandkids and always organized an Easter egg
hunt in her backyard. When I arrived, I'd help hide the plastic eggs. She
bought different colors for each grandkid. Dinner was spectacular—a
big ham with candied yams, creamed cauliflower, asparagus, and salmon
for those who didn't eat meat, and special dishes for the vegans and the
gluten-free.

This year, I was eating Easter dinner alone. I had scored fresh floun-
der from the Greenmarket at Abingdon Square, where I stood in line six
feet apart from my neighbors. My sister texted that she and her husband
were having Easter dinner for two.

"Who could have ever imagined this?" she wrote.

"It's like science fiction, but it's reality," I texted back.

I feel like we've gotten closer during this crisis. Easter morning, my
sister sent me a new recording by her daughter, Patty, who has a gorgeous voice. I hit play and heard my niece singing a cappella, "This is the
day the Lord has made. Let us rejoice and be glad."

As her sweet, clear soprano echoed through my loft, I was moved to
tears. The last time I saw my niece was on Christmas when she sang "O
Holy Night." When will I see my family again in person?

My nieces sent photos of their kids with their Easter baskets. And
that evening, we had a 45-minute family get-together on Google with
people living in four states: New York, New Jersey, Pennsylvania, and
Virginia.

I am touched by how people are helping in their own ways. Research
has shown that when you help people, you feel good about yourself,
creating what's known as helper's high.

I donated money so that Taim and Westville West, two of my favorite local restaurants, could feed the healthcare workers at Lenox Health
Greenwich Village and so the restaurants can stay in business. Others are
donating funds for laid-off workers at local restaurants. Or they're giving
money so healthcare providers can have PPE.

Many people are making masks. My friend Michele, a fellow writer, gave me a cool mask she created on her sewing machine. She was offering them free on Nextdoor. The Westbeth Beautification Committee is sewing masks, available free to residents and home attendants.

I've expanded my exercise routine thanks to the many teachers who have produced free or low-cost programs with specific exercises for the pandemic. I've done yoga for years, but I've now discovered some yoga moves for immune health. I've also learned qi gong breathing to strengthen my lungs and my immunity.

I studied qi gong in the '80s when I lived in the East Village. Who knew I would be calling it up again? So, I start my day with 20 minutes of qi gong breathing, and then I take out my yoga mat. I'm grateful that I already had tools I can use during this time of crisis. For years, I've meditated every morning and tried to eat organic and whole foods. From my yoga practice, I relax by doing deep three-part breathing.

As a writer who lives alone, I'm used to a solitary lifestyle. The problem right now is I don't have any companionship. I can't see my friends or family. I can't have a long chat with another resident in the lobby. On the occasions when I run into a neighbor on the sidewalk, our eyes connect above our masks, and we say hello, from a distance.

"Hey, did you see that Jenny won a Guggenheim?" I called to a Westbeth neighbor, a painter who teaches in the same NYU school as I do.

"Yeah, that's great," she replied.

I flashed back to us, laughing at the holiday party and sharing a cab back to our building. Now I wondered if my class scheduled for the fall will meet in person. Will anyone even have the money to spend on creative writing classes?

But September seems far away at this point. I'm just living from day to day, from week to week, living between the now and the not yet. I'm trying to stay healthy and focus on the good that is out there, like the kindness of strangers.

Melting Down in Lockdown

MAY 2020

I called my sister to wish her a happy Mother's Day. She has four daughters and many grandkids, ranging from young adults to a preschooler.

"I know this might sound crazy," I said, "but I'm really glad Mom is gone and not here for this."

My sister said that she was thinking the same thing. We would be so worried, even though our mother lived at home until she died at 95 in 2017. Later that day, I saw a post from a Facebook friend, a prolific author, who wrote she was glad her mother had died last fall. Many echoed this sentiment about their elderly parents.

My niece and her three girls went to the cemetery to place flowers on Mom's grave. My sister went later in the day, noting she was glad it was open, that it had previously been closed. I wondered why a cemetery would be closed.

"Too many funerals?" she guessed.

On Mother's Day, I made a donation to Eva's Village, my mother's favorite charity. It's an organization in my hometown in Paterson, New Jersey, that provides food and housing, rehabilitation, and job training to addicts. While their work model may have changed now, they are still supplying food to the hungry.

My mother was an incredibly resilient person, and I'm trying to draw strength from her during this difficult time. When I got my stimulus check, I donated a third of it to food banks and organizations helping to feed the healthcare workers.

In the workshop, my spiritual teacher asked us to make a list of 15 things that lifted our spirits. I discovered that donating money made me feel good. I enjoyed selecting the charities, making sure to include Sylvia's Place, which feeds the homeless LGBTQ kids.

When the lockdown first started, I was on a roll, writing five pieces within a few weeks. Then I fell into a slump. I had quarantine fatigue. I was depressed but reassured myself this was normal, given the circumstances.

I talked to colleagues on Facebook who also lacked the energy to write because they were so emotionally drained from dealing with the virus. I also knew others who remained prolific. I read articles about people having mental and emotional health issues. I wasn't alone.

Everything seems exhausting. Going for a walk is exhausting, as I get angry at the runners not wearing masks. Going grocery shopping is exhausting, as I worry if I've taken enough precautions. Going to the laundry room is exhausting, as I fear getting infected.

Of course, I'm taking the necessary measures—mask, gloves, relentless hand washing. After returning from my trip to the grocery store (I hit Brooklyn Fare during senior hour), I get home and wait for my delivery. I go downstairs to pick it up. I come back upstairs and clean my groceries. Then I feel exhausted. I'm done for the day—and it's only nine o'clock in the morning.

While waiting for my delivery, I quarantine myself in my "Covid chair" wearing my outdoor clothes. After I unpack the groceries, I strip off those clothes, toss them on that chair, and change into sweatpants.

Unlike those who escaped to houses outside the city, I don't have the luxury to wash my clothes every time I come back inside. I do laundry as seldom as possible. I'm wearing mismatching socks and bought more underwear online.

I believe that when this ends (assuming these folks return), New York will be divided into those who stayed and those who fled. No one outside the city can grasp what it is like here.

Even my reading has fallen off. I'm an avid reader who devours one or two books a week. During the winter, I read 28 books. (I keep a log.) This spring, I've only read four, including the classic *When Things Fall Apart: Heart Advice for Difficult Times* by Pema Chodron.

Much of my reading energy has switched to news. I consume newspapers online for about two hours every morning. I feel being informed gives me some small degree of control.

Since I retired from full-time teaching, I was working at home as a freelance writer, so my daily work routine has not changed much, except now I take classes and workshops online.

My reduced social life now consists of short conversations with my neighbors, either on the street or in the hallway (from a safe distance). On the other hand, I'd much rather be living alone in my cozy loft than with someone who drives me crazy. Through phone calls, I deepened friendships with people who enrich my life and make me feel less lonely.

As the lockdown drags on, I've had several meltdowns. One day, my Verizon Fios went out. Not having the internet scared me. I was shaking when I couldn't get a signal and saw the red light. I recalled that, in the past, unplugging it for a minute or two then re-plugging usually restored the connection. I did that and said a prayer. It came back!

Another time, my smartphone stopped working. I got a signal that it was overheated. I had never ever seen that before, and I freaked out. I called my computer-savvy contacts, grateful I still had a landline. I took it out of the case, put it aside for an hour. They said it would probably come back. After it did (more prayers), my 15-year-old grandnephew, an iPhone wiz, told me to turn down the brightness and delete any apps I'm not using.

The other meltdown came from a dental problem. A temporary crown cracked and fell apart. I took an ugly selfie and called my dentist. He thought it would hold up until he could see me. Told me to file down the jaggy edges.

My teeth need a cleaning, and my periodontist is not open. He is a miracle worker who managed to save many of my teeth. He is in his late 70s, so I hope he does not retire. I fear that after the lockdown ends, my teeth will be rotting out of my mouth.

Of course, I need a haircut and color, but that's not a big deal. Once I see my stylist, I will be fine. At least the rest of my health is good.

My worst meltdown occurred on a Sunday morning and caught me off-guard. I looked forward to watching church online. It gave me comfort and connection. On the last Sunday in April, the usual music came on before the actual service began.

As I heard the familiar song, "You're Welcome in This Place," I burst out crying and started sobbing hysterically. I put my head down on my desk and sobbed. I could not stop. I was crying for my lost life, which had been very good. I was crying because I have no idea how long this will go on and when I will be able to see family and friends again.

Normally, in May, I'm looking forward to going to the family beach house at the Jersey Shore and getting it ready for the summer season. I put that on hold this year and simply hope that I will be able to escape for a vacation in July or August.

Clinging to that thought keeps me going. I have no idea how I will get there—maybe car service—I don't care if it costs a fortune. I know that this season will be nothing like any other summer at the beach. During the two months here in lockdown, I've established routines that gave me some level of safety. I'd have to recreate that in another environment.

Now that we are fully into spring and produce is coming into the Greenmarkets, I'm walking to Union Square and shopping for fresh vegetables and buying plants for my garden at Westbeth. This is one of the few things that give me pleasure.

I also enjoy hanging out my window at seven o'clock every night and cheering and ringing a loud bell to commemorate city health workers. I love watching this family in this big building on West 12th Street. Their back terraces face my building. They come out every night at seven o'clock—Mom, Dad, three little kids. The kids and father are sitting and drumming like mad. The mother stands, shaking an instrument.

And I watch the neighbors across the street in a ten million dollar townhouse on Bethune Street. The father built a playground on his roof for his three boys, including a skateboard ramp and table tennis. At first, it struck me as the ultimate in "white privilege" while other kids are locked out of skate parks and playgrounds. But then I saw the father clapping for the workers, and he waved to me, and I liked him. Their housekeeper often sits on the steps and claps.

The clapping together brings us momentary joy in a time of deep sorrow and loss. Many are still dying, and the things that made New York fabulous are closed: the public libraries, museums and galleries, jazz clubs, theaters, restaurants. Crowded Hudson River Park is not relaxing.

Little did I know that when my sister took me to *Oklahoma!* on Broadway for my birthday in January (my friend's son played the lead), it would be the last time we would see a show.

Or the last time we'd see each other. I look at the Playbill and long for that life.

Kate's Westbeth Apartment, New York City, 2020

Gay Pride in Isolation

JUNE 2020

After I came out in 1975, I escaped from my conservative Catholic upbringing in New Jersey and moved to the East Village to be a dyke. Since then, I always mark the start of summer with Pride. But this year, the big NYC Pride March was canceled for the first time since 1970. Over the decades, I was thrilled to march and protest and cheer with friends and lovers. In 45 years, I have only missed this event twice.

I can trace my queer evolution from the different contingents I marched with over the decades. In the '70s, I stepped out with the feisty Lesbian Feminist Liberation. In the '80s, I marched with my partner as part of the Gay Teachers Association, where we met at a meeting. In the '90s, I went with the Gay Writers and was the group marshal. During the moment of silence, I thought of Joe, my college boyfriend who died of AIDS.

Of course, he wasn't my only loss. At the height of the AIDS epidemic, I protested with ACT-UP outside St. Patrick's Cathedral. (Rest in power, Larry Kramer.)

In the new century, I started marching with Middle Collegiate Church, which this recovering Catholic joined to get through the devastating breakup of my 26-year relationship. Reverend Dr. Jacqui Lewis, our pastor (who calls herself "the queerest straight Black woman"), led our loud group. We sang to the gospel choir, who rode on a colorful float.

I know I'm biased, but I think NYC Pride is the best—not just because I live here—but because we get to march past the Stonewall Inn, where it all began in 1969. Every year, the crowds roared as we headed up Christopher Street, past the legendary bar, where the sidewalks were jam-packed with bystanders waving rainbow flags and slapping our hands with high fives.

The Stonewall Inn had become a powerful international symbol of celebration and mourning. It was where we came to celebrate when gay marriage was declared legal, and Edie Windsor (a gay Rosa Parks) spoke to the ecstatic crowd. And it was where we came to mourn after the mass murder at the Pulse nightclub. Visitors from around the world stop here, like on a pilgrimage to a gay mecca.

Last year, in 2019, on the 50th anniversary of the Stonewall riots, two marches in New York City commemorated the event. The NYC Pride March went down Fifth Avenue loaded with glitzy floats from banks and phone carriers. Politicians and police officers stepped off to loud applause. More than five million people were on the streets for this huge celebration.

The alternative Queer Liberation March started in front of the Stonewall Inn and went up Sixth Avenue to Central Park, retracing the path of the very first one. This was a grassroots effort to reclaim Pride and return the parade to a community-based event. Corporate floats and police in uniforms were banned.

This more radical event attracted around 45,000 protesters. I attended with a group called Revolting Lesbians, organized by an NYU colleague. Over the years, I'd become disillusioned with the commercialized parade, but this new march re-energized me. I hoped both would continue—two marches in opposite directions.

I expected this year to be even more exciting since 2020 is the 50th anniversary.

As a senior gay woman living in Greenwich Village, I feel that gay elders like me are the keepers of queer history. I was upset to hear the coronavirus forced the community to cancel this annual weeklong celebration. No marches, no dances on the pier, no street fairs with vendors selling hot dogs and falafel and rainbow paraphernalia.

But then I learned the alternative march was back on for June 28, 2020, renamed the Queer Liberation March for Black Lives and Against Police Brutality. The city may be boarded up, but this protest will take place. But now, I was in a quandary. Should I attend? Is it too risky at my age? I'm healthy at 71 and don't want to get infected, especially after playing it safe for three months. And I certainly don't want to get shoved or knocked down.

In early June, Pride month began with a vigil at the Stonewall to honor queer people of color and other Black Americans lost to police violence. I wandered over, but the masked crowd was densely packed. I stood across the street but didn't linger. I couldn't hear the speakers.

The many safe Pride activities sound lonely and quiet. NYC Pride is hosting an event to be broadcast on June 28. Lambda Literary is offering a series of readings. Drag queens are doing bingo at home. DJs are holding virtual dance parties.

Will I be alone in my apartment dancing on Zoom? Having cocktails online with friends? Before the virus, I didn't mind being single, but it's harder with no real social life since March.

While I'm tempted, I think it's best to stay home from big marches. Let the younger folks take up the mantle for queer lives and Black lives. I've done my share of protesting over the decades.

I sent donations and took a two-part anti-racism master class taught by Reverend Jacqui. On June 19, Juneteenth, I attended a small Black Lives Matter prayer vigil outside Middle Collegiate Church.

On Sunday, June 28, I'll wear my rainbow bandana as my face mask and wave my rainbow flag from my window during the seven o'clock cheer, honoring the essential workers, especially those who are queer and people of color. And I'll cheer for the recent landmark Supreme Court ruling that protects LGBTQ employees in the workplace.

I may not be marching this year, but my Pride remains strong.

Kate at Queer Liberation March, 2019

The Walter Family Bungalow, Ocean Beach, New Jersey

Escaping to the Beach

SUMMER 2020

The one thing that kept me going during the spring was thinking that I would get to the Jersey Shore this summer. I was apprehensive about taking public transportation (New Jersey Transit), but I figured it was worth the risk to escape to the beach.

When I finally arrived, I was so happy. My brother John picked me up at the train station, the first time I'd seen him since last Christmas. John had grown a goatee during the lockdown, and his hair was longer. He looked good. He lives down the shore year-round, inland, over the bridge. A few days later, I saw my sister, Sheila, aka Sis, for the first time since my birthday in January. She has a summer cottage in a nearby community. I'm privileged to have inherited a vintage bungalow with access to a beach half a block away.

As soon as I dropped my luggage into my bedroom. I ran up the street to the beach walkway to see the little library in memory of my lifelong friend and neighbor, Sue, who died in August 2019 of a rare disease. The little library looked charming with its two doors with glass panels. The shelves were filled with books. Sue would have loved it. She was an avid reader and retired school librarian. We always exchanged novels. The library was my idea. I had suggested it during the homeowners meeting in the fall of 2019. I got teary-eyed when I saw the memorial plaque with her name.

I had been so lonely since the lockdown; I wished Sue was around to cheer me up. She was such a happy person. Her grandkids called her Happy, not Grandma or Nana.

Once the library idea had been approved, Sue's grandson took this on as part of his Eagle Scout project. It was built during the off-season and dedicated in early July. I was in the city then and missed the dedication ceremony. I took a photo of the library. As I walked back down our street, East Bay Way, I felt overwhelmed by loss, personal and global. I flashed back to three summers ago.

I pulled into the driveway returning from the hospital where my mother had just died. Even though Mom was 95, it was a shock because her mind was sharp, and she had been swimming in the bay with her great-grandkids a few weeks before. A month earlier, we'd sat on the beach reading our novels together. I'd taken Mom to dinner at her favorite seafood restaurant on the inlet in Point Pleasant. I couldn't believe I'd never speak to her again.

After Superstorm Sandy flooded the house, my steely Irish Catholic mother epitomized "Jersey Strong." When a crew of relatives tossed out furniture, rugs, and appliances, my mother donned rubber boots and supervised. She was so attached to our beach bungalow (and to my father) that when it had to be gutted after Sandy, Mom insisted that the repair crew take out and reinstall the knotty pine paneling my late father put in decades ago. I too loved the knotty pine.

As I stepped out of the car, I saw Sue coming out of her house across the street. I'd texted her that my mother was gone. She walked toward me with tears in her eyes, and we hugged in the middle of East Bay Way. Sue helped me get through that sad summer, 2017.

Sue and I grew up together at the Jersey Shore. We met when we were teenagers and used to write letters during the winter to keep up-to-date. When I cleaned out my childhood home, I found her "Sweet 16" birthday card. That cute tall guy she met one summer became her husband, Buz. I danced at their wedding. Sue married young and had three kids. I assumed Sue and I would become old lady friends like our widowed mothers, who used to drive to Atlantic City for dinner and the slot machines.

My friend had recently retired and was looking forward to my retiring so we could spend more time together at the beach in the fall. Then she got sick. It was so unfair.

Sue was diagnosed with a rare illness called multiple system atrophy. When we played Scrabble in my house, she now walked across the street with a cane supported by her husband, Buz. After the game was over, she called him to pick her up. (I didn't mind that she always won. I liked our conversation over the board.) We sat at the kitchen counter, a feature of all the old beach bungalows. Sue was very interested in my church and asked great questions about my writing and my debut book. During the next two years, she deteriorated.

The winter before she died, Sue sent me a friendship Valentine. She had never done that before. I guess she knew she was dying. When she called me in December, her voice was weak. When I last saw Sue in June 2019, she was in a wheelchair, sitting at the patio table in her yard, surrounded by friends and family. Her body was failing, but her mind never faltered.

While she was in hospice at her other home, she and her kids were watching 8mm home movies from the summer of '64. Her son asked me to identify some of the people. Who was Rick? (He was my high school boyfriend, who succumbed to AIDS.) Her daughter said I looked hot in a bikini. I agreed. I was tan, thin, and cute.

Her husband asked people to pray that Sue passes soon. She was too weak to even sip on a straw. She died at 70. We were born in the same year. Now my generation was going too.

"Makes it closer," said my therapist. "We're next."

During her celebration-of-life service at a beautiful old Protestant church in New Jersey, a speaker mentioned her friends from the beach community, who I spotted in the packed church. Sue planned the entire event herself. I choked up trying to make it through the Girl Scout song we did as a round: "Make new friends but keep the old. One is silver, and the other is gold."

When Buz visited me in my yard in the summer of 2020, it was obvious how much he missed his wife. When I'd pitched this memorial idea to the beach club, I had promised to tend the library, which her family had already stocked. I got into it, adding many books, moving the fiction to one section, the nonfiction to another, putting the children's books in a separate spot.

I made sure to include some novels Sue and I enjoyed together. I went daily to straighten up the books, which helped me feel connected.

Even though I really missed Sue, I enjoyed every minute at the beach: swimming in the ocean, riding my bike, eating outside at the patio table, entertaining guests in the little yard. I socialized more with friends and family in my first two weeks here than in four months in the city. It was such a relief to step outside the door and not have to put on a mask.

I heard live music several times, thanks to the beach club sponsoring concerts in the evening. I love outdoor concerts (and missed Summerstage in NYC), so this was a treat. The musicians were grateful to be working since the boardwalk clubs were closed. Every family group sat six feet apart, eating and drinking. My sister and I sipped rose and enjoyed a sultry vocalist who recalled Norah Jones. She got such a great reception; she played longer than scheduled. As the sun set behind the singer and her guitarist, I wanted to linger in this moment of freedom, like the endless summer.

I was dreading the idea of returning to Manhattan and experiencing what I did last winter and spring. Once it got cold, I wouldn't be able to picnic in the park as I did in June and July. I never liked sidewalk dining and had even less interest now. I feared my life would be almost like it was in April (very lonely), except now stores are open so I can buy books at The Strand.

But there still will be no fun group activities in the community room, no openings in our in-house gallery, no collegial in-person writing workshops, no hugging when we pass the peace in church. It will just be me alone in my apartment reading and writing and Zooming.

With fall coming soon, I get upset whenever I read a piece in the real estate section about homeowners fixing up their decks or porches or patios and getting heaters or fire pits so they can hang outside more in the cold. When the weather turns cool, I will be stuck back inside. Will the second lockdown be lonelier than the first?

I'm going to scream if I read one more piece about how the lockdown brought someone closer to her husband or wife or kids or parents. A colleague wrote that she was nostalgic for family time now that her husband was going back to work part-time. There was nothing positive about the quarantine for me.

Whenever I hear or read about anyone expressing anything positive about this situation, it feels like toxic positivity that makes me feel invisible. I have not hugged anyone since February. So please don't tell me how wonderful it was that you slowed down or bonded with people in your pod. Yes, I did reconnect with a high school friend, and I savor our regular phone calls, but it's still long-distance.

Years ago, when I went through a horrible breakup of my long-term relationship, I was distraught. I was angry. I was sad, but I didn't feel this aching loneliness, exacerbated by the fact that there is no end in sight. I don't want to return to that painful state again.

I'm not looking forward to the holidays. I'm afraid we will not be getting together as a family for Thanksgiving or Christmas, just as we did not meet at Easter. I will be lonely if I don't get to see my sibs and my nieces and their kids for our traditional feasts in New Jersey. There will be no fun party in the Westbeth community room with dinner and dancing to a live band. No joyful caroling in the lobby.

My therapist says I need to have plans for the fall and winter. Last spring, I taught myself to play the harmonica and got pretty good. When I played outside in the yard at the beach, the women renting the house across the street liked it. (Granted, they had been drinking.) I considered taking up the ukulele, but since I can't keep my guitar in tune, that may not work.

Before this plague destroyed life as I knew it, I was happy and thriving and seeing lots of people. I took all this for granted.

Now I'm in limbo. My life in New York City is on hold.

I kept reviewing what I had lost. Before the pandemic, I had a fantastic social life for a 71-year-old gay woman living in Manhattan. I missed my vocal group, "the Bliss Singers," that met every Friday. We sang blues and pop and show tunes and danced around the Westbeth community room to "When the Saints Go Marching In." I made new friends and felt rejuvenated when I left the session. Our teacher moved the group online, but Zoom does not work for singing together since we have to mute ourselves. Now I'm singing alone in my apartment.

Every Thursday night, I took the bus to a creative writing workshop in my friend Susan Shapiro's fabulous apartment in Greenwich Village. I've been in this workshop for more than 20 years, and it had become like a family. We celebrated weddings, birthdays, book publications. Now we meet on Zoom, which works fine, but I haven't seen anyone from the group in person since March.

Another thing that sustained me was attending services on Sundays at Middle Collegiate Church, a social-justice church in the East Village. I've been a member for more than ten years. The music was a big attraction: the gospel choir rocking a spiritual or the traditional choir with stellar harmonies or a Broadway star making a guest appearance. The sermons were always inspiring. My fellow congregants in this multiracial

LGBTQ-positive church were warm and loving, lots of hugging. Then I'd go to the social hall for brunch and conversation.

I miss being in the sanctuary hearing live music. Sometimes I start crying when I watch online and see performances I'd seen in person. I look for myself in the pews.

From the middle of March until the end of June, I socialized with exactly two people. (I'm not counting brief conversations with neighbors.) I shared a glass of wine with my neighbor on her birthday. I brought a peach cake from the Greenmarket. We sat six feet away in her apartment. And we met one other time. My colleague from the community college rode her bike down to my building to visit me, and we hung out in the courtyard, eating delicious falafels she picked up. That was it. Three interactions.

It was such a relief to get away to the beach and interact with more people.

Sue's Library

Coming Out Again at 71

SEPTEMBER 2020

I was disappointed when my 50-year college reunion was postponed because of the pandemic. I'd graduated from a small Catholic women's college in New Jersey, and the class of 1970 was slated to be honored at the school's annual homecoming weekend in the fall.

Then I got a request from my alumni association asking me to describe my life since graduation—"Fifty Years in 100 Words"—an update that would go out to my classmates. Yikes! If I wanted them to know me now, I needed to come out again at 71 years old. Hard to believe that, at this age, I was still strategizing about the best way to come out. This process never ended.

I was surprisingly anxious. I didn't want to be censored, although maybe that was an unrealistic fear. After all, it was 2020. But this was a Catholic school where the homecoming always included a mass at Rosary Hall. I did not recall ever seeing any same-sex marriage announcements in the alumni bulletin.

We were having a virtual reunion and creating this blurb was part of it. What did I want these women to know about me? I looked at the sample statements the alumni office sent us. One woman talked about how her Catholic faith had gotten her through the death of her husband. In other samples, people mentioned their careers or listed the names and ages of their children and grandchildren.

I had been single for over a decade and had no kids or grandkids. I was living alone, childfree and retired from teaching. What did my life add up to now?

I was no longer a practicing Catholic, although I had joined a social justice church that welcomes LGBTQ members. Unlike some of my classmates, I was not wealthy or a world traveler. I did not winter in Palm Beach and was not leaving an endowment to my alma mater.

Since I dated men during college, I definitely wanted my classmates to know I had become a card-carrying lesbian, although the ones I'd stayed in contact with already knew that; I'd hung out with a few of my sorority sisters ten years ago at our 40th reunion, skipping the mass at Rosary Hall.

After leaving the campus then, we had our private party at my friend's condo, eating delicious Italian food and drinking wine. We went through the yearbook, laughing and regaling each other with stories. I felt comfortable with this small group of women.

But now, that information would be going out to everyone on the email list, including that super sarcastic blonde bully from my class. I had to figure out the best way to work my queerness into my entry. No wonder I was nervous.

Everyone wanted their classmates to see them as a success, whether that meant producing books or babies, raising children, or mentoring students. I didn't have any children, but I had grateful students who thanked me every semester.

Many of my students were recent immigrants or first-generation Americans and the first in their families to attend college. I'd done important work in New York City for over 25 years. I helped my students improve their English and guided them through post-graduation plans. I encouraged them to become citizens and register to vote.

I approached this impossible life summary as a challenge. I decided to start in 1975 when I came out and moved to New York; I felt like my independent adult life started then. I didn't include anything about post-college life in New Jersey in the early '70s. While many classmates married right after graduation and started families, I was living with roommates in a big house on a lake, playing guitar in a garage band, and teaching high school English in my hometown.

Even if I'd wanted to, I could not say I was married and divorced because my 26-year lesbian relationship ended before same-sex marriage was legal. I did not miss the irony in that. I was left broke and broken-hearted, but I rebounded and created a happy life.

My religious parents were initially upset about my being gay. Yet both came around over the years, especially my widowed mother, who really helped me after the devastating breakup. No way to fit all that drama into 100 words.

It seemed too obvious to state how my bachelor's degree in English gave me a good foundation for my career as a writer and teacher. I mentioned my graduate degree and listed my two main jobs since I moved to New York City: teaching creative writing as an adjunct at NYU and teaching full-time at the Borough of Manhattan Community College.

I proudly included that I'd published a queer memoir. (That was how I subtly got in the fact I'm gay.) I gave the title and noted that my book was available on Amazon (a not-so-subtle plug to buy it). If they wanted info about my personal life, they could read my memoir. I included my website. I ended by saying that I was grateful to live in Westbeth Artists Housing in Greenwich Village.

I proofread my thumbnail autobiography, did a word count (101 words), and hit send. Days later, I got the copy back from the alumni office staffer editing this project. My piece was running basically unchanged, under my name and college yearbook photo (which she loved). My attire captured the era.

In this black-and-white photo, I'm in the local park sitting on a rock. I'm wearing bell-bottoms and a pea coat. I look very young. In 50 years, I'd come a long way from writing music reviews of Jefferson Airplane and Joni Mitchell for the college paper. Looking back, I found my calling while working on campus as a student journalist in the late '60s.

Like a modern queer version of *It's a Wonderful Life*, I realized I was very lucky. I had my health, good friends, and a loving family. I had supportive colleagues and caring neighbors. I had a beautiful rent-stabilized loft in a lively artist community. I had a full life and felt grateful. I looked forward to reuniting with my classmates in 2021.

As I sat in the beach house at my laptop and agonized over the blurb, I recalled the day that photo was taken. My classmate Jenny and I had driven to the park in her two-seat sports car. As we waited for the photographer to arrive, we smoked a joint to get in the mood for posing.

Years later, I heard through the girlfriend grapevine that Jenny, the biggest druggie on campus, had become a born-again Christian. She told a classmate that I was going to hell for being gay. I definitely think she took too many acid trips. I wonder if she ever got back her sanity. She had been brainwashed, like people who believed the lies of Trump.

PROUD PARENT OF A CHILD WHO
F*CKING HATES DONALD TRUMP

Seen in Westbeth during the pandemic, 2020

Return from Trump Land

FALL, 2020

"Hey, Kate, welcome back," said my neighbor in the hallway of Westbeth.

We were friends from the singing group. As we chatted, the first thing I noticed was her Biden-Harris mask. That made me feel good. I had just returned from a long stay in Trump Land in Ocean County on the Jersey Shore.

Earlier that morning, my left-wing friend Gerry had driven me to the train station in Bay Head. As we rode along Route 35 North, I noticed many yard signs for Trump and lots of banners flying from houses. They had increased since August. It was now the end of September.

"What happened to your Biden sign?" Gerry asked when she pulled up in front of my house. I had taken it down because my conservative niece was coming the next day with her kids, and I didn't want to upset an already fragile relationship. She and her husband are the only Trump supporters in my family. Gerry thought I should've left it up to needle her.

Two weeks earlier, I'd asked Gerry to bring over a Biden sign. (It was actually a bumper sticker that I taped into my window.) What prompted me was when the house in front had been rented to a bunch of Trumpers with New Jersey and Connecticut license plates.

As soon as they arrived, they tossed a big Trumpy party (with awful country music). One female guest opened up her car trunk filled with signs. She handed her hosts one: "I Stand for the Flag and I Kneel for the Cross." They put it in front of their rented house. That did it. I had to counteract this.

Although they did take down the silly signs when the party ended, I still had to walk past their cars with Trump bumper stickers. I saw them

giving my house the side-eye when they went past it the next morning and saw my Biden-Harris sign. Even though the Trumpers left, I'm
planning to put the sign back up when I return in mid-October.

I want to get a Biden-Harris mask to wear when I go into Rite Aid
in Lavallette, the local town. The first time I saw some guy wearing a
Trump hat in Rite Aid, we were standing in the aisle in front of the dairy
products. (Everyone I saw wearing a Trump hat was a white male.)

I couldn't control myself. "Trump is a racist," I blurted out.

"Oh, yeah?" he retorted. "If Biden wins, we will become a commu-
nist country."

"You really drank the Kool-Aid," I replied as I headed to the register.

On my last evening, I went to see the moon over the ocean. As I
turned to walk up the ramp, I saw an older white man sitting on a bench
with a Trump visor. The *New York Times* had just run that big story about
his taxes.

"Trump is going to jail," I said and stomped off.

"Why are you doing this?" asked my therapist, worried about my
safety. I told her I hate Trump, and it offends me that people are walking
around wearing these hats in the county where I grew up as a summer resident. They can wear their stupid hats and visors, but they're not
getting away without me commenting. Maybe if I get the Biden-Harris
mask, I'll be able to keep my mouth shut.

I have often wondered how my ultra-liberal friend Gerry can live
in such a conservative area year-round. But people are attracted to the
area's natural beauty. Gerry loves the beach life and still goes boogie
boarding at 78!

Barnegat Island is a narrow strip of land between the bay and the
ocean, and the beaches are beautiful. That's what attracted my parents so
many years ago. It was also an affordable area for them to buy a bungalow in a small summer community.

When my mother died three years ago, my siblings and I inherited
the house in Ocean Beach that my parents bought in 1949. I'm glad my
mother lived long enough to vote for Hillary. Mom and Gerry used to
play Scrabble together.

Ocean County was always solidly Republican in terms of the people who live there year-round. The second-home owners tend to be

Democrats from North Jersey or New York City. As more people from North Jersey relocate to Ocean County year-round, the demographics are changing. My liberal brother moved his family there many years ago. He, too, hates Trump.

When I was living in the bungalow during the month of September, I noticed way more people than usual were around because they are working remotely and their kids are going to school remotely. I wondered if some would decide to relocate permanently.

Considering the changing demographics, I would have expected to see a few more Biden signs. During my bike rides, I saw only one while I was blinded by houses with two or three Trump banners blaring from their rooftops. Very ostentatious. Maybe they feel a need to do this because New Jersey is a blue state.

It's always a culture shock staying in Ocean County since I live in Greenwich Village. But this year, it was more intense. As I walked the hallways of Westbeth and visited the courtyard, I felt grateful for the warm "welcome home" greetings from neighbors and staff. And I felt grateful to live in New York City.

I'm still dreading winter, but at least I won't see any Trump hats in the Rite Aid on Hudson Street.

NYC trashcan, November 2020

The Day Biden Won

NOVEMBER 2020

The weather in Manhattan was warm on Saturday, November 7, around 65 degrees. I woke up wishing I was at the beach house instead of in the city that weekend. But then I would've been in Trump Land when the media announced Biden's victory. Looking back, I was so happy I had stayed in the Village.

That morning I had volunteered to plant tulip bulbs in Christopher Park, across the street from the Stonewall Inn. The park is now part of the Stonewall National Monument. I enjoy urban gardening, and there was nothing more to do with the two boxes I tend outside my building. So I jumped at this opportunity to dig in the soil. As usual, I entertained the idea I might meet someone. I'd responded to a call for volunteers posted on a neighborhood website.

I threw on ratty jeans, old sneakers, a down vest and walked over to Christopher Street. When I got to the park, I introduced myself to the head gardener who was opening up boxes and boxes of tulip bulbs. I signed into the volunteer log, took a bottle of water, gloves, and a spade from a supply table. I was early and did a little clean-up. I picked up litter and threw it into a plastic bag: cans, bottles, candy wrappers. People were really slobs.

Other gardeners started to arrive; they seemed to know each other, but this was my first time. I said hello, and then the head gardener assigned several of us to a southwest section of the park near Seventh Avenue. We spaced out. Of course, we were all wearing masks.

I knelt down in the soil and started digging and planting the tulip bulbs as instructed. Bending over like this was harder on my back than I expected, so I'd stand up to stretch and have a drink of water. The soil was muddy, and my jeans were getting filthy.

I was probably working a little over an hour when all of a sudden, I saw a group of people whooping and shouting as they walked up Christopher Street past the legendary Stonewall bar.

"What happened?" another gardener called across to them.

"Biden won!" they shouted back.

"They called Pennsylvania."

I dropped my spade and stood up and pumped my fist in the air and started screaming, "Yes, yes, yes." I was so happy and relieved. LGBTQ Americans would have support and recognition from the federal government, and all states could expect a smooth rollout of the vaccine.

Sheridan Square had gotten busy since I'd arrived. It was Saturday morning, a gorgeous fall day. Locals were doing errands and going out for brunch. People walking by on Seventh Avenue asked what happened. Word spread fast.

Now cars and cabs and trucks were going down Seventh Avenue, honking their horns. A man stood in front of the Monster, a gay bar on the corner across from the park, and intoned solemnly, like a newscaster: "Joseph R. Biden has just been declared the 46th president of the United States. Joseph R. Biden has just been declared the 46th president of United States."

People were going crazy as the word continued to spread. I couldn't manage a better place to be than in Sheridan Square in front of the Stonewall Inn in the heart of Greenwich Village when I heard this news.

I worked for a bit longer: planting tulip bulbs, then getting up and clapping, planting and standing up, screaming and waving to the crowds. When I emptied out that box of bulbs, I decided to go home and get cleaned up. I handed in my gloves and spade and signed out.

When I got back to the far West Village, I saw crowds around the Greenmarket in Abingdon Square. People were yelling and clapping as cars headed up Hudson Street honking. A man standing on the corner in front of the farmer's market opened a bottle of champagne. A tap dancer in a tuxedo was working the crowd on the corner across from the market. I went home, took a shower, changed my clothes, charged my phone, and got ready to go out and party.

This was the happiest I had been since before the pandemic. Finally, I felt hopeful. I don't think I could've continued if Trump had won. I was seriously thinking of getting my EU citizenship. (I qualify because my mother was born in Ireland.) I could sublet my place and move as soon as I was able to travel. Now I could stay here in New York and in America, my home.

At some point, I checked my email. I knew my cousin Eileen would be celebrating.(She does not text.) She lives in Pennsylvania and had worked really hard to win voters over to Biden. This was her message:

Hi Kate, It's official! The Mad King is dead; long live the President-Elect. Our long national nightmare is finally over. I hope that a small plane is flying over the golf course right now, with a banner the monster can see, which reads: "LOSER"!!!

I can hardly believe it. Are people dancing in the streets there? Ringing bells? I wish that I had fireworks. I know that it's only noon, but we have a bottle of champagne waiting out in the garage fridge that we didn't get to open four years ago, ready for this moment.

Thank God, and God bless the American people for rising to the account and making their voices heard in record numbers. Love and celebration,

Ei

I wrote back describing the super festive scene in the Village.

She replied: *Wish I were there. Playing "Save the Country" over and over, which has been going through my head for weeks.*

I told her I also loved that Laura Nyro song. (We were both baby boomers who grew up on the same music). It had been in my mind too.

I headed back to Sheridan Square. The block on Christopher Street in front of the Stonewall Inn was where we celebrated victories and mourned losses. Today was a huge victory.

The street was now closed off to traffic, and masked crowds were milling around. The bar had set up bistro tables outside, and revelers with Biden-Harris signs and shirts were drinking and toasting. A man and woman, either a straight couple or two friends, each had a champagne bottle. They popped the corks simultaneously and swigged. The crowd roared.

A huge stereo speaker was blasting music out of a window of a high-rise building next to the bar. I imagined this person was a frustrated DJ who had not worked in the last eight months. "Celebrate good times, come on," sang Kool and the Gang. "There's a party going on right here."

Yes, it was a party, and we were here for it. At some point (maybe it was after Queen did "We Are the Champions"), the DJ segued into Sinatra singing "New York, New York." How perfect, and we were so ready.

When Frank built up to "These little town blues are melting away," the crowd was waving and swaying as we anticipated the next few lines. Yes, we were all a part of it in New York, New York, on this wonderful, historic day.

Celebrating Biden's Victory, Stonewall National Monument, NYC, November 2020

The Pandemic Changed Me: I Learned to Like Clothes Shopping

NOVEMBER 2020

It would be ironic if the pandemic made me get over my aversion to clothes shopping. Eight months into the pandemic, the things that I really enjoy in Manhattan are still not available. I can't attend concerts or plays or hang out at the Cubbyhole. I can't go dancing.

Other than walking in Hudson River Park, what can I do for fun? I can eat in a sidewalk cafe (when it's warm enough). Or I can bop around SoHo or Chelsea or Union Square or the East Village and look in stores.

Last fall, when I saw a blurb in the newspaper for pile-lined sweatpants at Uniqlo, I wanted to stock up before the cold weather. And this is one of the few clothing stores I don't totally hate. I like the store layout and their cool T-shirts with artistic prints.

So I planned an expedition to SoHo to hit Uniqlo for sweatpants and McNally Jackson for books. I had a gift certificate for this cool indie store, and I like shopping for books.

The first thing I did after New York reopened was go to The Strand, Barnes & Noble, and Three Lives. I had a great time at the tiny Three Lives. I discussed books with another customer and got recommendations from a salesclerk. I had missed that.

But there is no way I missed clothes shopping. My dislike dates back to my childhood when I was a girl and my mother dragged me with her from store to store on Main Street in downtown Paterson, New Jersey. Back in the '50s and '60s, before the suburban malls, my home city had a lively commercial area with department stores and specialty shops.

I felt trapped. I wanted to be playing basketball or roller skating, but I was forced to help my mother decide on patterns and materials for dresses she would sew. (Not the least bit appealing to a tomboy.) I was bored after half an hour, but my mother wanted to shop much longer. I couldn't wait to get home. The only thing that kept me going was the reward.

When we finished, we went to the soda fountain at Woolworth's, and I ordered a hot fudge sundae with whipped cream and sprinkles. I plopped down on the spinning stools, trying to restrain myself from twirling while waiting. I was an energetic baby dyke in training.

No surprise, I've never had an extensive wardrobe. If I can buy stuff online, like shoes or sneakers, all the better. I keep buying the same foot-wear in different colors. I also buy socks and underwear online.

My former partner, a fashion plate, loved shopping and tried to ex-plain why she enjoyed it.

"Buying makes people feel good. They like having new clothes. May-be you don't get shopping because you're not into having things," she observed about my simple, unadorned lifestyle.

"Or maybe I'm not into having things because then I'd have to shop for them," I retorted.

Before I went to Uniqlo, I did the size chart online. I was a large. But when I got there, they only had white in large. I wanted a dark color, like black or navy. The salesclerk said she thought I could wear a medium, noting that she wore a large (and she was a lot bigger than me.) So I took a chance and bought the medium in black. The dressing rooms were closed due to the pandemic. As soon as I got home, I tried them on; they felt tight in the inseam. If they shrunk, I was in trouble.

If there's one thing I hate more than buying, it's returning. The next day, I revisited the store, hoping Uniqlo might've gotten a new shipment overnight. A different clerk told me that they had more pile-lined sweat-pants in a slightly different style in another section.

Since I live alone, I was desperate for an in-person conversation with anyone about anything. I actually enjoyed talking to the store clerks about styles and sizes, colors and fabrics. What was happening to me? Was I turning into my mother? I found my size in royal blue and was all set. I forced myself to leave before I started going through racks and buying stuff I did not need.

Due to the exchange, I made two clothes-shopping trips to SoHo in one week—something I would have hated under normal circumstances. But as I walked down Broadway, I realized I wasn't as bothered by this as I'd expected. For starters, Broadway was not packed with rich European tourists hitting the many shops. I could actually walk on the sidewalks.

During my first trip, I even felt a little sad when I noticed all the boarded-up storefronts and "Space For Rent" signs. I never thought I'd miss the days of bustling SoHo. As I went back the second time, I realized that I enjoyed walking down Broadway and looking in the store windows. Going back to Uniqlo was not so awful.

Besides new sweatpants, I needed a fleece-lined hoodie to replace my favorite because the zipper broke. I went looking the day after Thanksgiving, not even realizing it was Black Friday until I got to Paragon and saw the sale signs outside. Never in my life have I gone shopping on Black Friday. I used to make fun of the people who did.

I thought the store might be packed, but there were almost as many clerks as customers. Paragon only had zippered sweatshirts with brand names, so I went to Old Navy, which was a little busier but not crowded. I bought a $35 hoodie and paid $17.50—on sale with 50 percent off.

As I stood in line to pay, I started having an anxiety attack. No one was ahead of me, but the two cashiers seemed to be taking forever to ring up their customers. I felt sweaty, overdressed for an unseasonably warm fall day. Was I freaking out because I feared the virus, or did waiting in line to buy clothes take me back to childhood?

Everyone was masked, and the guy behind me kept his social distance. Yet I could not wait to pay and get outside. I wondered if I was taking too much risk to buy a sweatshirt.

But if I wanted to try it on, I had to visit a store. With a little more practice, this could become my winter entertainment.

After I got home, I needed a relaxing walk in the park. I threw on my stylish blue sweatpants and my gray hoodie. I looked fashionable. So, this was why people liked shopping.

Took me a lifetime—and a pandemic—but I finally got it!

The next time I go hunting for clothes, I'll end my trip at the Big Gay Ice Cream shop in the Village and order an old-school hot fudge sundae.

My Pandemic Dreams

NOVEMBER 2020

And the dreams kept coming, the crazy dreams and nightmares. I had been sleeping poorly since the City went on lockdown, waking up at 3:00 or 4:00 a.m. with a nightmare. My sleep was better during the summer when I was at the beach, but once I came back and the virus spiked again in the fall, the scary dreams resumed. At least now, when I woke up, I did not hear sirens screaming through the night as I did last spring.

I legel believed that the "zeitgeist" of a time period is reflected in our dreams. No surprise many people were having pandemic nightmares. I always had lucid dreams, and I was glad I could discuss these new ones with my therapist. In November, I had three scary dreams:

I got off the subway at 72nd Street and walked through the glass doors. I entered a corridor, like a tunnel. I was drinking a beer and threw the can into a dumpster. But when I got outside, it was lower Manhattan, not on the Upper West Side. Now I was on Broadway between Great Jones Street and Bond Street in NoHo.

I heard sirens and people screaming. I looked up, and this building was on fire. Then, everywhere I looked, buildings were on fire, absolutely everywhere. It was very scary. I started to run, thinking I should call someone and let them know I'm okay.

"The fire is the virus," said my therapist, Dr. R., as if it was obvious. "The virus is everywhere, and you want to escape."

"Didn't you use that subway stop when you saw me on the Upper West Side?" she recalled.

"Yes, I did," I said, connecting the dots. "And the other location in NoHo was near your office when I saw you on Mercer Street in that high rise."

Was I running to Dr. R's office to escape the virus? For sure, therapy with her was helping me cope with my anxiety. I had been seeing Dr. R for decades in various locations.

The next pandemic dream: *My doctor wanted me to take this pill—or was it in an injection—that would kill me so I would not get the coronavirus. I was supposed to take it in a couple of days. "But I don't want to die," I argued. "I'm only 32."*

I countered that I'd rather take the risk of getting Covid, and most people who got it did not die. The doctor in the dream looked like my pastor, Reverend Jacqui.

"That whole scenario makes no sense," I said to Dr. R. "What does it mean?"

"You feel scared," said Dr. R. "You're not afraid when you are awake, but you feel it when you're sleeping. You worry about everyday choices. Try your best to take as little risk as possible."

The third dream from November:

I'm lying on the sidewalk on Washington Street near Westbeth. I'm sunbathing and surrounded by guys asking about the height of this nearby building. I answer them, and then one leers over me. The others leave, and I'm scared. I think I may get raped. This guy has missing front teeth, and he spits onto my face. I tried to scream and push him away. Then I wake up.

This was a vivid dream where my sleep paralysis kicked in. (I finally learned the name for it.) My mind wakes up before my body. I'm awake in my room, but I can't move. I'm frozen in fear.

"You're napping on the sidewalk like a homeless person, and the toothless guy seems like a homeless person," said Dr. R.

I told Dr. R that I'd just seen a picture of a toothless person celebrating in Washington Square Park after Biden had been declared the winner. I remembered that when I went to the beach during the summer, I was unnerved by the homeless people running around Penn Station without masks. I felt vulnerable as I stood there with my luggage, six feet away from the other commuters, waiting for my train to be called.

"I should be sunbathing in the park or on the beach, not on the sidewalk," I said. "Maybe I feel displaced since I got back to the city. Like I'm in the wrong place."

"You felt less scared at the beach," noted Dr. R. "You slept better.

There's no escaping now that you are back. You can't get away."

I later found out that my publisher also had a pandemic dream about multiple fires that took place on Bond Street. We felt this was synchronicity. And I wondered if the fire dream was a premonition of the awful church fire that occurred the next month.

My Beloved Church Burns Down

DECEMBER 2020

As if this year could not get any worse, my house of worship burned down early Saturday morning, December 5. My friend texted me, saying she hoped it was not my church. It was.

I started crying when I saw the videos of the flames roaring through the roof of Middle Collegiate Church on Second Avenue. I've been a member of Middle Church for 12 years.

I joined after I went through a devastating gay breakup. Attending services at Middle helped me rebuild my life and get back in touch with my spiritual side. I felt so calm in the sanctuary with its beautiful Tiffany stained-glass windows. The sanctuary was completely destroyed, all the windows were blown out.

Led by the dynamic senior minister Reverend Dr. Jacqueline Lewis, Middle Church welcomes everyone and has a large LGBTQ membership. It is one of the most progressive churches in the city and was on the frontlines in the fight for marriage equality. It even sponsors a float in the Gay Pride parade. A few months ago, I attended a Black Lives Matter vigil out in front of the more-than-century-old edifice (built in 1892).

Reverend Jacqui prayed, and we responded. About 50 of us, socially distanced and wearing masks, kneeled or stood in silence for more than eight minutes. Then we stood up and chanted "Black Lives Matter" as cars going down Second Avenue honked in support.

Middle Church participated in the women's marches in New York and DC and sponsored the annual Revolutionary Love conference, attracting people of faith from around the country. We commemorated the murder of Trayvon Martin by all wearing hoodies to church. The Sunday after Trump won, the pews were packed. The choir sang, "Jesus is a rock in a weary land, a shelter in a time of storm." Before the election, we sent thousands of postcards to voters.

What always struck me about the congregation was its diversity. It is racially, ethnically, culturally, and economically diverse. Someone wrote on Facebook that one time when she went to services at Middle Church, a homeless person sat to her left, and a celebrity was on her right.

I think it's fair to say there is no other congregation in New York City like Middle Collegiate Church. Its motto is, "Welcoming, Artistic, Inclusive, Bold." As a recovering Catholic, who fled a homophobic church, I felt at home and embraced.

With its two choirs—a classical choir and a rocking gospel choir—the music was amazing. So was the dancing on the altar and up and down the aisles. Attending a service was like going to a Broadway show. In fact, some singers who soloed there, like Tituss Burgess, are Broadway performers.

Several years ago, on Christmas Eve, I took two Jewish friends. They loved the music and thought Reverend Jacqui was "a rock star." Like our new VP Kamala Harris, Reverend Jacqui and her husband are an interracial couple. (She's Black. He's white.)

When, five years ago, the NYPD and FDNY spent weeks clearing the site of the terrible gas explosion fire across the street, Middle Church opened its social hall as a spot for city personnel to use its bathrooms and have food and coffee. With the church's roots dating back to the colonial period, this tragedy is a loss to all of New York City but especially the East Village.

We have been meeting online during the pandemic, and we were all looking forward to when we would be able to get back inside our church next year. The last person I hugged before the lockdown was a fellow congregant.

We were supposed to have communion outside on Sunday, December 6, the first Sunday of the month, a new tradition recently started. Last spring, we lost the sanctuary to the virus, but it was still there waiting for us to return. Now, it's completely gone.

On the night of the fire, the church held a Zoom meeting, "A Time to Grieve, A Time to Mourn." More than 500 people attended, and people from all over the country wrote in to the chat to offer support. I was struggling to believe; then Reverend Jacqui issued a message, "No fire can stop Revolutionary Love."

Amen.

Ministers outside Middle Collegiate Church on Second Avenue, October 2020

Middle Collegiate Church after the fire, December 2020

Rita Houston: The DJ Who Saved My Life

DECEMBER 2020

This was a terrible year, and December was a terrible month. First, my church burned down in a six-alarm fire on December 5. Then, my favorite DJ Rita Houston, whose Friday night show "The Whole Wide World" on WFUV got me through the lockdown, lost her six-year battle to cancer on December 15.

I felt like I spent the month of December crying. I cried when I saw the video of Middle Collegiate Church burning. I cried when I was home alone on Christmas Eve watching the service from Middle Church that was broadcast nationally two years ago. I was in the sanctuary when they filmed it.

I loved when the choir led the congregation in singing "Silent Night." We held lit candles and the sanctuary lights dimmed. Knowing that I would never be in that space again felt unbearably sad. The broadcast was updated with Reverend Jacqui Lewis, the senior minister, looking radiant and talking about how we would rise up and rebuild.

A week earlier, I was anticipating Rita Houston's radio show. I never missed it. She hadn't been on the air the past two weeks, and I hoped she was on vacation. That afternoon I read the newsletter from the station and learned she had died that week. The station sent condolences to her wife, Laura Fedele, who also worked there. How did I not know Rita was gay?

That evening, Friday, December 18, WFUV broadcast her last show, recorded a few weeks previously and co-hosted with her friend Paul Cavalconte. I was mesmerized. What would she play? How would she say farewell to her listeners and to her life? Her familiar, deep, honeyed voice did not sound good. I was crying and dancing, kicking myself for never going to the station's holiday concerts at the Beacon Theatre, where she was the host.

Now Rita Houston was gone, too. She was only 59. I considered her program another sanctuary. Her voice was reassuring and calming, always around when I needed her. She was there when I went through a terrible breakup and when my mother died. And more recently, she was there during the lockdown in New York when I was really scared at the beginning. I recall her playing Van Morrison's "Till We Get the Healing Done" and thinking what a great choice it was. Of course, that was before Morrison turned into an idiotic anti-mask nut.

Music is a huge part of my life. I listen to the radio and read books. I don't even own a TV. I send checks to my favorite public radio stations. I admit my fantasy job was being a DJ on the radio. The closest I got was working as a music reviewer for many magazines and newspapers.

Like me, Rita Houston grew up in the New York City area, listening to the legendary DJs Alison Steele and Vin Scelsa and Frankie Crocker, whom she cited as her influences. Houston was known for her eclectic mix and introducing listeners to new artists from around the globe. She was the first to play Brandi Carlile on the air.

Among her favorite artists were Bowie and Prince and John Prine and Sharon Jones. She also loved Joni Mitchell and Lucinda Williams and Rickie Lee Jones. And she had an incredible knowledge of '70s and '80s disco. Last summer, when she played the classic "Last Night a DJ Saved My Life" by Indeep, I tweeted to her that she was saving mine. She retweeted me.

Houston could go from folk to funk or from alternative rock to disco in a heartbeat. Her mix and segues were brilliant. She was also a great interviewer.

The station website has the entire playlist of her last show. Her final mix included several personal favorites: "The Weight" by the Band and "I'll Take You There" by Mavis Staples. And a remake of Roy Ayers' soulful classic, "Everybody Loves the Sunshine." She closed with "In My Time on Earth" by The Waterboys. By now, I was sobbing.

Besides the loss to her family and friends, Houston's death is a huge loss to music lovers and to WFUV, where she was the program director. She had revamped the station, taking it from a folkie venue to a showcase of different sounds and genres. She was on the air for 26 years. Hard to believe I will never hear another new show from her. I was a huge fan. She made Friday night fun.

Home Alone for Christmas

DECEMBER 2020

I was spending Christmas alone for the first time in my entire life. My family had decided to play it safe. We were not getting together in a large group. We were listening to Dr. Fauci. My sister sent me a beautiful poinsettia plant from her and her husband. She felt bad I was alone.

Normally I'd be at my niece's beautiful lake house in New Jersey. She had taken over hosting Christmas dinner after my mother reluctantly gave this up in her last years.

Christmas at Monica's home looked like a photo spread from a Martha Stewart magazine: huge tree in the living room with gifts underneath, fireplace roaring. Stockings hung from the fireplace mantle, with a Nativity set on top.

As everyone arrived, we had drinks and snacks: chips, dips, crackers, cheese. Then we sat down for a sumptuous dinner—turkey with all the trimmings, salmon, and lots of side dishes, mashed potatoes, sweet potatoes, green beans, turnips. We adults ate on the sun porch at a long table set with Christmas china. The kids sat at a table in the dining room.

After dinner and the dishes were cleared, the kids carried in the plum pudding, made weeks before with my grandfather's recipe from Ireland. Years ago, my nieces brought in the pudding; now, the ritual had passed to their children. The lights were dimmed, the whiskey poured on top, and someone flicked a lighter. As the kids marched carefully from the kitchen, with the flaming pudding on a tray, everyone had phones or cameras ready to take pictures.

I never ate the plum pudding because I hate raisins, and the pudding contains suet. Luckily, dessert also included apple crisp and an assortment of homemade Christmas cookies, the same ones my mother used to make.

I grew up with family legends around the pudding. If it cracked when the cheesecloth wrapping was peeled off on Christmas Day, someone at the table would die within the next year. My mother recalled that the pudding cracked the Christmas before Aunt Mamie died. However, it did not crack the year before my father died, so I dismissed this as morbid Irish folklore. Yet, everyone present always held our breath when the pudding was unwrapped.

Later, we crowded into the living room, and the kids went crazy opening presents. After the mess of wrapping paper was picked up, we sang carols around the piano. My sister played, but the highlight of last year was when my grandniece (then in fifth grade) did a little recital—a solo on the "Carol of the Bells." The song has a wide range of notes, using keys from both ends of the keyboard. It was hilarious when she dramatically slid from one end of the piano bench to the other (to reach the notes) and ended with a flourish. We all applauded like mad.

Unfortunately, her piano lessons ended because of the pandemic. We would not be gathering at the table this year or standing around the piano to sing. So much for our holiday traditions.

I decided to give myself a vegetarian holiday feast. I looked up recipes and found sweet smoked apple and sage sausages with roasted vegetables: potatoes, apples, and red onions. It turned out fabulous, but I made a lot of food and needed a serving dish. So I reached into the top shelf of my kitchen cabinet and took down dishes from a set I had inherited when we cleaned out my childhood home in New Jersey.

I'd never used these dishes, but this was a special occasion. I spread the food out on the serving dish, took a picture, and texted it to my family.

"The potatoes look like grandma used to make," texted my niece.

"Loved those dishes," texted my sister. "They were my favorite."

That evening, we had a short family get-together on Zoom.

As I made preparations for Christmas alone, I remembered the other festivities from last year: my neighbor's wonderful Hanukkah/winter solstice party where we lit the menorah, and someone chanted in Hebrew. I also recalled the feast that I went to on the next block. It was hard to believe that a year ago I was at a family dinner party and two other parties with many people packed into Greenwich Village apartments. I'd dubbed one of them "the old party."

The Old Party

DECEMBER 2019

Since I wanted to have one more great relationship before I died, I pushed myself to attend parties, events, workshops. Even if I didn't meet Ms. Right, I craved good conversation since I lived alone and worked at home.

I was excited when my new friend, Nadine, invited me to her holiday party. Even better, she lived around the corner. We'd met in my singing group. Both altos, we sat next to each other every week, trying to stay on key.

I walked in with a bottle of hard apple cider, and Nadine greeted me with a hug, noting that I was dressed up, not in my usual outfit of sweatpants and sneakers. It was Christmas Eve, and I'd just come from church. Nadine was Jewish and told me she'd started this party years ago "so the Jews would have someplace to go on this night."

As I sized up the space—it was pretty crowded—I immediately noticed that everyone was old. Almost everyone looked over 70, and lots of people appeared to be in their 80s. I guessed Nadine to be in her late 60s, her husband a bit older. I saw a number of guests wearing hearing aids. Oh. No. I was at "the old party." What was I doing here?

I had never gone to a Manhattan soiree where everyone was my age or older. The hosts' Asian son, who seemed around 30, really stood out—no surprise he made an early exit.

Everyone was old. Everyone was white. Was everyone straight? If there were other queer people there, I missed them—and this party was in the West Village. I wondered if all the gay men in this age bracket had died of AIDS (like my friends and colleagues). I was used to going to parties with more diversity—the beauty of living in New York City.

I was tempted to slip out discreetly until I saw the food table. It was spectacular—a whole turkey with dressing, an entire ham. And many choices for us vegetarians: green salads, curried wild rice, latkes with sour cream and apple sauce. Lots of wine and eggnog.

I filled my plate with salads and roasted veggies and found a chair. Everyone was super friendly—no attitude. I really liked my host, and her guests seemed warm, like her. My usual conversation openers for a party in the City are "Where do you live?" and "What do you do?" Most people were from the West Village or the Upper West Side. I imagined that, like me, they landed in Manhattan before the City cost a fortune. I was thankful I had moved here when New York City was still affordable.

I hesitated to ask the second question assuming most people were retired. But wait a minute. I was retired from my full-time teaching job, and I was still working as a freelancer and an adjunct. Why was my concept of my fellow guests so limited? For all I knew, these folks could be taking art classes, studying Italian, traveling, sky diving, volunteering, or still working. Why was I buying into this ageist crap?

My mother lived to be 95, in good health and kept going because she wanted to see her nine great-grandchildren grow up and celebrate their milestones. While I had no kids, being older gave me a deeper perspective, especially on neighborhood issues. I liked helping younger students who studied with me, and I was thrilled when they sold their first pieces.

I chatted with a woman who wrote for the local paper who was pleased I knew her byline. She was younger than me, in her 50s. "I've read your coverage of the empty storefronts and small businesses closing and what we can do to stop this trend," I said. "Good work."

I met a male psychologist who was also a rapper. A senior rapper with rhymes about toxic masculinity! It looked like he was trying to pick up my neighbor, a talented photographer who lives in my building. She was also in our singing group and one of the two people I knew at the party, other than my host, who was flitting back and forth from the kitchen to her company. When I explained to other guests how I'd met Nadine, that started a conversation.

"What kind of songs do you sing? Do you perform?" I was asked.

"Everything from the Beatles to Gershwin to gospel," I said, realizing we had a big repertoire. "We had a gig singing carols, and we're practicing for another event. Our teacher is great, so energetic." (Never mind that she was around my age.)

What was different about being at the "old party"? No one was judging me. No one was trying to impress me. So that felt relaxed. I had a good time. If anyone was sizing people up by their age, it was I, and I needed to grow up and stop that. And accept that I was old too.

Holiday decorations at Chelsea Market, December 2020

Brief Encounters of the Pandemic Kind

WINTER 2021

Iused to have a vibrant social life. I met friends for lunch. I went to parties, art openings, readings, workshops. I drank wine and mingled and chatted with people. I'm an extrovert who has no problem going into a social situation and striking up a conversation. I'm a funny storyteller. I like talking and meeting new people.

I was always chatty. My second-grade teacher told my mother I was the best reader in the class, but I talked too much.

But now, all my weekly meetings had moved online, and my downtown Manhattan social life disappeared. Instead, I had created a regular weekly schedule of Zoom classes, five or six a week: yoga, qi gong, meditation, writing, singing. I knew all the teachers and most of the students. Having a weekly routine with activities every day helped me cope. It was a good mixture of exercise workouts, artistic endeavors, and spirituality.

While I enjoyed speaking to friends on the phone or networking with colleagues in Zoom meetings, it was not the same as talking in person. It had become a thrill to chat in person, even with a clerk, even better if he or she knew my name. I now had to make do with the little scraps of conversation, the brief encounters on the sidewalk or in the hallway or a store. These moments took on more meaning. They became a lifeline rescuing me from solitude.

I was delighted when I ran into my neighbors Michele and Jonathan at the AIDS memorial listening to the audio presentation that ran through the month of December. Michele is in my singing class, but I hadn't seen her since the spring when she walked over to my building and gave me a mask she had sewed. Her hair had gotten so long!

I felt recharged when I ran into Isaac, the piano player from our choral group, in the chiropractor waiting room. He was coming out of his session while I was waiting for mine. It felt like old home week. I hadn't seen him in person since March, the last time we had a singing lesson in the community room.

Since I've been spending a fortune on books, I'm now taking advantage of "grab and go" at the New York Public Library. I reserve a book online and pick it up when it comes in. I was happy to chat with the librarian who recognized me (even with my mask on). She recalled me from another lifetime when I was a frequent patron who actually sat in the chairs and read books.

"How do you like working at Hudson Park?" I asked, trying to make conversation.

She was normally assigned to the Jefferson Market branch, but it was still closed. Very helpful, she searched online for a book I hadn't reserved and got it off the shelf for me. (Patrons are not allowed to browse.) I thanked her.

The first time I went there after the libraries reopened, I felt weird standing in front of the temperature-check machine before entering. Now I know exactly where to position myself and to take off my hat. But first, I toss any returns into a big tub. Then these books go into quarantine for a few days. (I'd asked why books I had returned still came up online as checked out.)

I'm excited when the hip clerk in Sea Grape, my favorite wine store, says, "Hey Kate. How's it going?" Even though I usually buy the same two wines, I linger and ask for recommendations since he knows my taste and price range.

I'm so desperate for company that I actually look forward to going to my chatty periodontist. Never thought I'd say that about getting my gums scraped and cleaned. Not only has this brilliant dentist saved my bad teeth, but he's a lovely older gay man, witty and cultured. He invests in plays, knows a lot about the theater in New York and London, and riffs about old movies. He's a Vietnam vet who hates Trump and loves Nancy Pelosi (although he felt her face was pulled too tight). Needless to say, he does most of the talking, but I enjoy listening.

When I saw him in October in his office on the Upper West Side, we were worried about who'd win the election. When I saw him in January (after the inauguration), we were both thrilled but appalled at what happened in the Capitol on January 6.

I also discussed the inauguration with the physical therapist helping me with the tendonitis in my ankle and calf. I was moved by Lady Gaga's version of the national anthem, although it was a far cry from when she sang it at a Pride rally in TriBeCa and changed the words to "and the land of the free and the home of the gay." I basically assume all my health care providers in Manhattan hate Trump. My physical therapist, a young woman fresh out of grad school, underscored this as we discussed John Legend's soulful performance.

I'd been anxious about going back to my chiropractor in December, but severe ankle pain drove me there. He said the pain was not caused by sciatica (which he'd treated in the past) and told me to see a medical doctor. So I saw my sports medicine specialist. He diagnosed tendonitis and prescribed ibuprofen and sessions with his physical therapists. I had been there years ago for various problems. By comparison, the place was very quiet. I did as few sessions as possible.

Most days, my neighbors or the building staff are the only people I speak to in person. I appreciate their regular friendly greetings. I bask in the brief conversations in the hallways or elevators. A painter shared that she had a show last February, then the lockdown occurred, and the exhibit closed. She didn't sell anything. I commiserated.

When the pandemic started, we were only allowed one person at a time in the elevator. After several months, we were allowed two at a time in the elevator. Between the masks and winter hats, we sometimes relied upon voice recognition to know who said hello. "Is that you, Joan?" Sometimes I identified my masked neighbors by their dogs.

This was better than riding solo, but it still wasn't like the old days. I missed the packed elevator conversations, including when someone gossiped about the person who'd just stepped off. "That guy never says hello to anyone."

But some tenants had to push this relaxed rule instead of being satisfied. One day, I was on the elevator with a neighbor having a good conversation. The door opened, and someone asked, "May I get on?"

"No, full house," I said, but she got on anyway.

Now there were three of us on the elevator. We went down to another floor, and a fourth person got on. I said, "This is too many. I'm getting off."

I stomped out and walked downstairs to the lobby. I was already cranky, and this inconsiderate behavior pushed me over the edge.

Then there were individuals who got on without even asking when there were already two of us on board. I'm not in that much of a hurry that I would jeopardize my health or that of my fellow residents. At least all these offenders wore masks.

I looked forward to chance encounters when out for my daily walks or running errands. I enjoyed this "happenstance" as Fran Lebowitz called this in an article in *New York* magazine.

Early morning was a popular time to run into neighbors walking their dogs. I bumped into Jean, a former colleague from the community college. She lived across the street and introduced me to her new dog. Also walking her dog was Carol, the woman who used to work at the desk of Integral Yoga Institute, where I took classes for years. Even though I was doing yoga at home, I missed the soothing vibe of the yoga center with its beautiful rooms and mandalas on the walls.

One Sunday morning, when I went out to buy the *New York Times*, I ran into a member of my church in the supermarket on the corner. We discussed the fire and how we're sad the church burned down a month ago. He looked on the positive side and pointed out how it's great that we've had services online for the past ten months. Then he said, as I turned to walk away, "Don't worry. We will be back."

These brief encounters give me hope. They remind me of the life I used to have and will someday have again.

Scheduling the Vaccine on My Pandemic Birthday

JANUARY 2021

I was so desperate that I started praying to my dead parents: "Mom and Dad, please help me to get an appointment." The next time, after starting the registration process all over again, I picked February 12. I got to the end. "Please, please, please let this work," I was praying as I hit "Submit." And it went through! Yes! Thank you, thank you, Mom and Dad. I knew they'd want me to protect myself. I had managed to schedule a vaccine appointment, a month later, at the Javits Center.

After this horrible year had finally ended, all I wanted was to get the vaccine. As soon as I saw that the shot was available for people over 65 (as opposed to over 75), I jumped on this. I thought it was a good sign that the day the state made this announcement also happened to be my birthday, January 12. Getting this appointment on my birthday was a great gift from me to me. But I had to be persistent.

I went on the government website, filled out the questions to find out if I was eligible. (I knew I was, but that was part of the procedure.) Then I typed in my zip code and went to a list of places offering the vaccine. I skipped those that required a phone call because I knew it would be impossible to get through. I went to the Javits Center website, thinking they'd have a lot of slots daily, and I don't live that far. It's a short bus ride from my corner. So I'd pick a date and time, answer all the questions. Or was it the other way around?

I'd do all this, get to the end, and then the site kept crashing before I could hit submit. Sometimes it crashed before I got to submit. This went on for a couple of hours. I was getting frustrated, and I was looking at the time. That's when I started praying.

I had a haircut and color at 4:00 p.m. in Chelsea. I had to leave my apartment by at least 3:30 to get there on time. But I had to nail this life-saving appointment before I left. If I didn't, hundreds of time slots would be gone. During the hours I'd been working the site, I could see the dates disappearing like mad.

But I finally got through. Then I got an email with the registration from the New York State Department of Health. I printed it out. It looked like a ticket I'd get if I were scheduling a show through Eventbrite. I had a coveted ticket for an event at the Javits Center—my vaccination. Now all I had to do was stay safe for another month. I worried whenever I went to an appointment and kept them to a minimum. I could walk to the salon in Chelsea, less worrisome than taking a cab or bus.

I was seeing Heather, my long-time hairstylist in Mane Space, where she had set up shop after leaving her job at a big fancy salon in NoHo. She didn't feel safe working in a busy place. Mane Space was like We-Work for hairstylists. Each person had her own private cubicle, so it felt very safe. This was the second time I was going there and the first time I was getting color in a year.

It was just Heather and me in her mini salon nook. She was now a one-woman shop. She washed, cut, colored. She even swept the floor herself. I am very risk-adverse. I would never go to a big salon. Nor would I eat inside a restaurant. But I was doing this one thing for me to lift my mood. Plus, later in January, I was on a Zoom panel from the Strand Bookstore, and I wanted to look good. I didn't have that much gray, but getting color (lowlights) made my hair pop.

Heather was thrilled when I told her I had gotten an appointment for the vaccine. She had to wait because she was only 50. She was careful. She only saw her husband, her pod members, and clients. My first time there, she took my picture with the mask after she finished the cut.

It was a treat to sit in the chair and talk to her for over an hour. The last time I had an in-person conversation of that length was during the summer at the beach. She too despised Trump, and we worried about the upcoming inauguration, especially after what had happened on January 6. She said she was sorry she could not get me a birthday cake.

When I left Mane Space, I stopped at a health food store and bought myself some tofu strawberry shortcake. That night, I spoke to my sister and brother, who called to wish me a happy birthday. Three nieces texted me. Knowing she would not see me in January, my sister got me an early present during the summer: a backpack beach chair, the cool new beach accessory. By now, almost everyone in my family had celebrated a pandemic birthday.

Her card arrived on time, but my brother's card came a week late because the mail was screwed up due to the pandemic. His card was really sweet. It said, "I am proud of you, of your grace, your wisdom, and your accomplishments."

Hopefully, my sister and I could get together next year for dinner and a show. Broadway was still dark, and indoor dining was canceled. New York was cold and dreary. But I was in the home stretch.

I had this dream in January after I scheduled the appointment: *I'm driving a car on a drawbridge. It looks like the Mantoloking Bridge at the Jersey Shore. (I went over this bridge a lot to get from the beach house to visit my mother in the hospital in Brick, where she died.)*

The bridge goes up while my car is on it. I'm hitting the brakes, but I'm about to go over the edge. The bridge is going up-up-up. The car flies over. It is terrifying, but instead of landing in the water, now it's like I'm inside a video game I used to play in a beach arcade. I'm driving and keep steering the car on the road.

"It reminds me of a cartoon," says Dr. R. "Like when someone gets bonked on the head, sees stars but gets back up. Catastrophe befalls you, but you survive. You have to keep steering. It's a nice ending how you keep the car on the road."

"What's the bridge represent?" I mused aloud in the session. "A bridge is a connector, but a connector to what? Is it pre-pandemic and post-pandemic?"

"Will we ever get to the other side?" Dr. R. said dramatically.

Revising My Pandemic Routines

FEBRUARY 2021

Over the past year, as I learned more about the virus and how it was transmitted, I changed my routines. I no longer washed my groceries. I no longer wore indoor and outdoor clothes. I basically wore the same clothes all day (sweatpants). I no longer wore plastic gloves in the laundry room or the grocery store, but I wiped down the shopping cart whenever I went grocery shopping. I used the sanitizers in the stores and around my building. I carried sanitizer with me, and I washed my hands religiously. (That ritual had not changed.)

I went from wearing no mask to one mask to two masks as the virus dragged on and stronger new variants appeared. I put on an extra mask before I entered a store. I envied people who lived in suburbia or the country who could walk outside their door without a mask to their yard or car. (One of the best parts of being at the beach house was not having to wear a mask as soon as I stepped outside.)

Back in Westbeth, I even put on a mask to walk down the hall to the incinerator. I put on a mask before I left my apartment and didn't remove it until I returned. I loved the poster I'd seen stapled to a pole in my neighborhood: "Real New Yorkers Wear Masks." Like most downtown residents, I was now wearing the black surgical mask, which *New York* magazine deemed "the new fashion statement."

Back in the spring, when we first were told to wear a mask, everyone was scrambling to find face coverings, exchanging news on the website Nextdoor about what stores carried masks. Now I had boxes of surgical masks and several cloth ones, even a mask from Village Preservation with an iconic black and white photo that said, "Save the Village."

After I washed the cloth masks, I put them on my radiator to dry.

I started buying boxes of black surgical masks from vendors at Union Square who had the best prices. And I could see what they looked like, as opposed to buying online, where I bought some crappy black ones I had to return. While I'm all for supporting local businesses, I resented the price gouging at a nearby store, where I'd bought my first box of black masks. I'd become a mask bargain hunter.

When the pandemic first started, everyone was hustling to get bottles of Purell. They were sold out in the stores, and I bought two overpriced bottles online. Now I scored little bottles of hand sanitizer in Staples, on sale for $0.99 each. I popped them in my coat pockets and in the tote bags I used for shopping.

I'm saving my bottle of New York State Clean hand sanitizer (made by inmates in correction facilities at the beginning of the pandemic to address a shortage). It will be a collector's item. I don't think they were sold in stores. I got mine free in a care package from my state senator. In my role as floor captain, I helped distribute them in my building.

In the beginning, I stocked up on Tylenol and cough decongestant and bought an oral thermometer. I still took my temperature a lot and worried every time I had a sniffle or scratchy throat. But I don't think I'd call this corona phobia. I never got tested.

Hitting the Wall

FEBRUARY 2021

I watched church live streamed every Sunday. On February 7, the start of Black History Month, Reverend Jacqui preached a sermon echoing the theme, "I am so tired. I'm tired in my bones. My body hurts. My head hurts."

Reverend Jacqui rolled on. She was tired of the pandemic. Tired of the violence against Black bodies. Tired of the political shenanigans. Tired of how January 6 was brushed over. Tired of how America works. Tired of Zoom. Tired of having the same conversations over and over.

While the online services were comforting, I missed seeing Reverend Jacqui walk out onto the altar. She was an attractive woman, a great dresser who alternated from colorful ministerial robes to power suits, from high heels to boots. Her fashionable wardrobe and changing hairstyles caused gay men to gush as she entered the sanctuary, "Oh my God. She looks fabulous."

Jacqui was a charismatic preacher. I missed seeing her leave the altar during an emotional sermon and walk up and down the middle aisle, tears filling her eyes as she wrapped up with a dramatic conclusion.

It was two months since the church had burned down and almost 11 months since we'd met inside the sanctuary. Donations to the rebuilding fund had already topped over a million dollars. The insurance policy covered 20 million, but it would probably cost many millions more than that to rebuild and furnish a church sanctuary in New York City.

I didn't know how Jacqui did it. It had to be difficult (even with a great staff and supportive husband). She was dealing with the full-time work of the fire: comforting her grieving congregation and focusing on rebuilding. She had to fit all that into the regular church ministry (now totally virtual) while Covid loomed as the backdrop.

In addition, Jacqui wrote and sold a book during the pandemic: *Fierce Love: A Bold Path to Ferocious Courage and Rule-Breaking Kindness that Can Heal the World* (Penguin Random House: November 2021). She said this was the hardest she'd ever worked since the first year when she came to Middle Collegiate Church.

But clearly, her faith got her through, and a loving community held her up.

"God is not exhausted," she preached, "and promises rejuvenation and restoration."

I totally related to feeling tired and worn out and I did not have many responsibilities. I was tired of wearing a mask, tired of the cold and snow, tired of being alone, tired of not being touched or hugged. I missed my friends and family and desperately wanted a massage. I walked regularly, but the sidewalks were gross with piles of dirty snow and recycling piled on the mounds. The sanitation budget had been cut, and people had gotten careless about picking up after their dogs.

After 11 months of this, I felt I was hitting the proverbial wall. I hoped that getting the vaccination would perk up my mood and get me to the finish line. At least I'd feel less anxious about getting sick. I tried to focus on gratitude as a way to get through the wall.

I was financially secure. I lived in a rent-stabilized building in a desirable neighborhood. I had my writing, a key to my survival. I toyed with the idea of going back online to try and meet someone but decided to wait until the spring when we could meet outside in the park.

At this service in February, we improvised communion in our respective homes to honor the 400,000 people who had died of Covid. I had a cracker and fruit juice. And I made a donation to the rebuilding fund. Volunteers were helping to arrange vaccine appointments and the church was supporting those struggling to pay their bills due to Covid.

In her blessing at the end, Reverend Jacqui reassured us, "We're gonna make it."

Getting the Vaccine

FEBRUARY 2021

A month passed since I made the appointment. It was February 12, my V-Day. I got up early and checked the weather. It was 21 degrees, cold but no wind, so I'd be okay waiting for the bus. I left with time to spare. I was always early and organized. That was my personality.

The night before, I laid out everything I needed: my driver's license, insurance cards, and the important registration form confirming my appointment. I'd printed it out, but it was also on my phone. I packed two good luck charms—vintage jewelry that belonged to my parents: my father's tie clip and my mother's four-leaf clover pin. The last time I had taken them with me was when I did a reading at the Westbeth community room on March 4, right before the lockdown. I couldn't believe how much time had passed since then. A year of anxiety.

I caught the M11 bus on the corner, took it up Tenth Avenue, and got out at 34th Street. Now I had to walk to the Javits Center, past many construction sites where the icy sidewalks had not been shoveled. I was really careful, at one point going into the street. The last thing I needed was to slip and fall while the vaccination center was literally within sight.

The entire procedure at the Javits Center was smooth and efficient, run like a precise military operation. Polite young men and women from the New York State National Guard directed us, "Turn left at that soldier," "Turn right at that soldier." It is the largest vaccination center in the country.

When I arrived, I waited five minutes until I was waved to a check-in station, where I handed in my forms, showed my ID, and answered questions. When I got up from my seat, a soldier directed me where to go next. I walked the length of two blocks to the vaccination area. To my right, I saw a guardsman wheeling a woman in a wheelchair.

The Javits Center is huge. I flashed back to the last time I was here—for Book Expo America. At the vaccination area, I waited until a soldier waved me to an empty station. I sat down. This was it!

"Hi, I'm Jessica," said a pregnant African American woman in blue medical scrubs who asked for ID and my consent before she jabbed me in my non-dominant arm.

"Hi, Jessica," I said.

I was almost crying now. I was so relieved. After I got the vaccination, another woman at this same station gave me a card with a date for my second shot. Then a soldier directed me to the rest area to sit on a folding chair for 15 minutes. I took a selfie of me wearing my sticker, "I Got My Covid-19 Vaccine at the Javits Center," and posted it to Facebook.

As I got up to leave, I realized I was in and out in less than an hour. I did not miss the irony that it took far more time to set up this appointment. This was incredibly smooth and efficient.

"Have a good one," said a cute female soldier as I headed toward the exit.

"You too," I said. "Thank you." I must have said thank you ten times during my visit.

For the past month, I'd read articles about how hard it was to make an appointment, how people were using various strategies. Luckily, I am a fairly tech-savvy senior with a great internet connection. When I got home, I texted my siblings the good news: I got the vaccine.

Meanwhile, out in New Jersey, my niece Monica was on a mission, hell-bent on getting appointments for her parents (both over 75). When she heard that CVS had the vaccine, she was up at 5:00 a.m., working on multiple computers, ready to pounce as soon as the drugstore portals opened. She was proud that she snared appointments for her parents, although my brother-in-law was going on Friday and my sister was going on Monday. My sister said that all 20,000 appointments disappeared within ten minutes. This is a race, and computer savvy plays a big part in who wins. My niece thought this system was unfair to seniors.

I felt a little tired on Friday when I got back from the Javits Center, but I figured it was the anxiety of getting there and back. The next day, Saturday, I felt completely exhausted, fatigued. I could barely make it to the grocery store. I spent the rest of the day on the couch reading the new Tana French novel *The Searcher.*

According to what I read, 62 percent of people who receive the Pfizer vaccine experience fatigue as a side effect. But that was it. My arm felt fine. I got a good night's sleep and woke up on Sunday feeling fine. I had my energy back.

My next appointment is on March 5. I heard it takes at least ten days to be fully effective, which would be March 15, my father's birthday. My parents are still looking out for me.

The Second Time Around

I felt a lot calmer when I went for my second shot at the Javits Center because I knew the drill. Call me superstitious. I wore the exact same clothes as the first time and packed my good luck charms again. It was still really cold at 25 degrees, but at least the snow and ice were gone.

The bus was waiting on the corner. I hopped on, and everything was fine until we'd gone about ten blocks, and some idiot boarded without a mask. (The driver said nothing.)After he sat down, I called out to him, "Put your mask on." He did, but not over his nose. I moved my seat.

When I got to the Javits Center, it was much more crowded than my first time. Now there were at least 100 people ahead of me, but the lines moved quickly, thanks to the New York State National Guard directing us. I saw lots of people who didn't look over 65. But in the last three weeks, more people had become eligible due to their medical conditions.

Yet I had numerous friends and colleagues in New York in their early 60s who didn't qualify for the vaccine. I felt bad for them. I also knew couples, like the gay men across the hall, where one qualified but the other didn't due to an age gap.

A healthy neighbor, who is 64, said, "It's the first time I ever wished I was older."

I shuffled along to the Muzak as we all maintained six feet apart. I was grateful to see a hydration station and grabbed a bottle of water. I amused myself looking at the line by guessing who lived in Manhattan and who lived in the outer boroughs. I decided the people with the skinny jeans and cool boots lived in Manhattan. The chubby guys wearing sneakers, ill-fitting jeans and shirts that said New York Rangers or New York Mets lived in Queens. I knew I was being a snob.

I wondered how people would tag me. I was wearing striped Adidas sweatpants, short black boots trimmed with faux fur, and a stylish black parka. *Manhattan*, I thought.

As I played my silly guessing game, I couldn't help but notice the majority of people moving along the line were white. I didn't know what to make of that.

This time, when I got to the check-in desk, the woman asked me for my insurance card. I was really glad I had brought my Medicare card. When I mentioned that no one asked me for this the first time, she said, "I'm doing my job properly."

I hoped she did not take it as a criticism.

"I like your shirt," I said as we finished up the registration. She was wearing a Black Lives Matter shirt.

"Thanks. Stay safe," she replied.

As the next line moved toward the vaccination area, I chatted with a couple behind me. I heard them wondering about reactions. I felt like an old hand, reassuring them that I had almost no reaction to the first shot except for some fatigue. No headache. No fever. No sore arm.

"That's great," the woman said.

When I got to the vaccination table, I commented to the intake worker that the center was a lot busier than three weeks ago.

"Yes," she agreed, adding, "now we are doing vaccinations 24/7, around the clock."

The way she said it, I got a sense that everyone at the Javits Center was proud to be part of this massive life-saving operation.

This time I was asked, "What qualifies you for the vaccine?" I thought that was odd because this was my second visit, and I wasn't asked the first time. But since then, the vaccination criteria had opened up. It was no longer limited to seniors.

"I'm over 65," I explained, although she had already asked my birthday when I handed her my license. Were people borrowing IDs? Was that why she checked my birthdate?

"You look great," she said.

She also asked, "What is your first name Ms. Walter?"

"Kate," I automatically replied, then quickly corrected myself, "I mean, Kathleen," knowing it had to match my legal name on my license. I wanted to get this right.

Then the nurse came to do my vaccination. When I told her this was my second shot, she said, "Congratulations."

I waited in the post-vaccination area for 15 minutes. As I headed toward the exit, I saw the "Thank You" bulletin board. I posted a message and went back out into the cold, humming, "Happy days are here again."

New York was doing a better job than New Jersey with rolling out the vaccine for people over 65. By the beginning of March, my brother and his wife, both over 65, were still unable to schedule the vaccine near their home in New Jersey. He said they were registered in a bunch of places, and he checked every day for openings. But there were none. Same story with two couples who were friends of my sister and all over 75. They could not get appointments.

I had two shots before my brother and sister-in-law even got their first ones. At least my sister and brother-in-law had managed to nail appointments thanks to my niece's over-the-top computer efforts.

Despite the emergence of the vaccine, the pandemic was far from over. Both New Jersey and New York were adding coronavirus cases at rates higher than the rest of the country. Or maybe the red states were not counting all the numbers.

In late February, a popular Westbeth tenant, who was near 90, died of Covid. He was still active in our community before the building went into lockdown. My grandnephew, who lives in Bushwick, had to go into quarantine when his roommate tested positive.

Biden predicted that by the end of May, every adult who wanted a vaccine could get one. I thought he was doing a great job getting needles into arms. So was Cuomo.

Rooting for Hudson Street

MARCH 2021

I was in a good mood as I turned down Hudson Street and headed to the post office. The snow was gone, and spring was coming. I'd been vaccinated and felt ready for the city to reopen.

But then I walked past Golden Rabbit and felt sad, immediately reminded of all that had been lost during the pandemic. My favorite mom-and-pop store was another Covid casualty.

Golden Rabbit was a little stationery and party supply shop owned by a friendly immigrant couple. I always went there for computer paper, cards, flowers. This loss was deeply felt by the community, especially my neighbors who were parents. They fondly recalled buying party supplies for their kids when they were growing up.

When the owners put a sign in the window announcing a closing sale, I stopped by to pick up a few items and wish them luck. I'd heard they put their daughter through law school from working long hours in the store.

The rent was high. I was amazed they had survived for decades. I assumed they stayed in business by selling lotto and scratch-card tickets and renting mailboxes. The store was small, even smaller than I had realized. When I walked past the space, now gutted, I could not imagine how they had crammed so much inside.

As I continued along Hudson Street, the main drag in my neighborhood, I counted 15 empty storefronts with signs, "Retail space for rent." All within a few short blocks. It was depressing.

Hudson Street has a history: Jane Jacobs was a resident, living a few doors from the White Horse Tavern. I read that Diane Arbus took some iconic photos on Hudson Street. That makes sense since she lived nearby in the newly opened Westbeth, where she committed suicide in 1971.

As a New Yorker, I was used to seeing businesses close but not so many within a year. How would I manage without Teich? I bought presents for my grandnieces and nephews in this upscale toy store; they had a variety of arts and craft kits and did lovely gift wrapping. Teich saved me on many occasions, like when I was rushing out to a birthday party.

Restaurants were especially hard hit. Philip Marie had been on Hudson Street for many years. Now a sign in the window said, "Thanks for the memories."

I regret never dining at the Filipino Taqueria when it was still open. I also never made it to Kish Kash, which specialized in couscous and opened in 2018 to rave reviews.

I missed the pizza place where I stopped for a slice on the way back from the Hudson Park Library. The kids from PS3 loved that spot and jammed in there after school. Their high energy made me glad I never taught elementary school. Of course, the bad pizza place on the busy corner that attracted unsavory characters had survived.

Small businesses gave the neighborhood character. They made me feel like I wasn't living in a big city. Kathleen, the owner of the tiny Manhattan Mailboxes on West 12th Street (thankfully still open), always greeted me by name. She was very kind after my mother died when I needed her to notarize a lot of forms.

Right next door to Manhattan Mailboxes is Grove Drugs, where I get prescriptions filled. Before the pandemic, the pharmacist conducted wellness programs in the community room of my building, and the staff always brought gift bags with samples of body lotions. Free swag. Rite Aid and CVS never did that.

Even the chains have been hit: Starbucks on the corner of Hudson and West 10th Streets shut down. And the Verizon store where I'd gotten help with my phone.

Bleecker Street, which had become overrun with high-end designer shops, was also lined with empty storefronts. This started even before the lockdown. I can't say I was upset. Bleecker Street had completely changed from when I moved here in 1997, and those blocks still had local shops.

The three nearby liquor stores on Hudson Street were all thriving. (During the lockdown, I started ordering wine by the case from Sea

Grape.) I'm sure I drank more with all this wine stocked in my apartment. I was lonely, and there was little else to do.

Restaurants were trying to survive after setting up stalls with heaters for outdoor dining during the winter. Some had closed but promised to reopen in the warmer weather. My last time sitting at a restaurant table was outside the Bus Stop Café on a mild day in November.

The Bus Stop Café, an institution on my corner, was still hanging on though I had not been inside in over a year. I used to eat breakfast there all the time, sitting in a booth by the window. The waitstaff knew my order. Coffee, two eggs over easy, wholewheat toast, butter on the side. That seemed like a long time ago.

I remembered how the Bus Stop Café reopened right after Sandy with a limited menu. I think they were using a generator. My neighbors and I waited in line to get inside. We shared tables and ate by candlelight.

Back in 1997, when I was finally offered an apartment in Westbeth Artists Housing, I ran up Bethune Street to the payphones outside the Bus Stop Café to spread the good news. After 22 years in the East Village, I was packing up and moving to the far West Village.

I was replacing funky Second Avenue with the more upscale Hudson Street. I was anxious about uprooting. I'd identified strongly with the East Village (where I'd moved from the hippie house in New Jersey when I was 25). I wondered if I could be happy across town.

But over the past 24 years, the far West Village, with its weird, confusing street grid, had become my home. I was comfortable here. I bought fish and cheese and vegetables at the small Greenmarket at Abingdon Square every Saturday. I loved being ten minutes away from Hudson River Park. I couldn't imagine living anywhere else. Although I was far from rich, I'd played my cards right and landed up in this desirable neighborhood.

But what would my neighborhood look like when this was over? The Partnership for New York predicted that when the pandemic subsides, one-third of the city's small businesses would never reopen. I was glad when NYS passed a bill providing massive Covid relief (one billion) to help small businesses recover, but it was too late for many.

I had a fantasy that commercial rents would drop and attract new entrepreneurs. We could reset the clock and reverse the gentrification that catered to tourists and wealthy newcomers. I envisioned more small businesses that served locals.

Or would the storefronts remain empty like that prime real estate on the corner of Sixth Avenue and 8th Street that used to house Barnes and Noble but had been vacant since 2012? If this happens, how would it impact the city's economy? I did not want to return to the 1980s.

People predicted that TriBeCa was finished after 9/11, but the neighborhood came back stronger than ever. But even Century 21, the iconic discount designer store that bravely emerged, dust-covered, after the terrorist attack, could not survive this current disaster. Many of its customers were tourists, who have vanished.

On the upside, as the pandemic continued, residential rents in Manhattan and Brooklyn dropped to the lowest in years, luring and retaining young people who could not have afforded to rent here in the past. My grandnephew, Casey, loves living in Bushwick, the new East Village for this generation. He moved there shortly before the pandemic and was able to hang onto his apartment because he got unemployment when the photography studio where he worked was forced to close.

I sensed a buzz in the air as March continued. This Irish woman was happy that Hudson Hound, a popular Irish American pub, reopened on St. Patrick's Day, serving pints of Guinness, fish and chips, ham and cabbage, and bangers and mash. Hudson Hound had closed for the winter, but it was back! I wanted to do a jig.

I stopped by for the craic (fun) and to toast my mother from County Cork. I met a friend, and we sat outside drinking beer and eating delicious chips. It was a chilly day, but the sidewalk tables were filling up, and the food looked great.

A few days earlier, I saw a sign in the window of Henrietta Hudson Bar and Girl, the lesbian bar in business for 30 years. They were reopening in the spring with plans for a stylish outdoor area in the parking lane: exclusive pods for guests and plenty of outdoor sidewalk seating. Maybe I could meet someone and we'd kiss in a pod. Years from now, I hoped I'd still be here, with Hudson Street thriving.

On the Verge of Reentry

SPRING 2021

After I was fully vaccinated, I felt more relaxed. My overall anxiety level dropped. But then my initial burst of euphoria over getting the vaccine tapered off. Now, what would it be like to wend my way back into a post-pandemic world? I had no grandkids to hug. I never liked flying, and I rarely took the subway, even before this plague. I planned to postpone indoor dining until more people were vaccinated, and now it was warm enough to sit outside.

What about those new variants? Even now, no one knew if those vaccinated could be carriers. I would continue to wear my mask.

Many of my activities would remain on Zoom, but my writing group was slated to resume in person again in the fall. We met in a private home, not a public space. It would be great to see everyone again. I loved this group, even when they trashed my first drafts.

Habits already in place had served me well—I'd meditated for years and kept a gratitude journal for a long time. But the biggest lifestyle change was that I learned how to cook. I had no choice and clipped recipes from the new "At Home" section of the *New York Times*. I developed a survival menu of soups, chili, burritos, pasta. I did weekly meal planning.

I was fortunate to have a well-stocked fridge and pantry. Many New Yorkers were hungry. Besides donating money, I dropped off canned goods or boxes of pasta at the food pantry outside St. Francis Church in Chelsea. One Sunday, there was a crowd of men standing on the sidewalk drinking coffee. As I placed a box on the pantry shelf, someone came up behind me and grabbed it immediately. Then this same guy pulled the next box from my hand as I took it from my tote bag. It didn't even get to the shelf. People were desperate.

This personal interaction underscored my privilege. Not everyone suffered equally. A lot was determined by class/race/gender. I passed long lines for free groceries at another church when I went to the health food store. Families were lined up, mothers with children. While I was riding the Fifth Avenue bus, I saw a man scarfing down a block of Kraft cheese, like he was starving.

I walked away from an unmasked homeless man begging aggressively at the Union Square Greenmarket. (He was asked to leave.) I saw a man rambling through a sidewalk café on Sixth Avenue, going from table to table, begging. I was used to seeing homeless people panhandling on the sidewalk in front of CVS or Starbucks, but the pandemic had made this more widespread. It would take years for New York City to recover from the unemployment and homeless crises. I planned to get back to activism and volunteering to help the renewal of my beloved city.

I'd struggled with insomnia during the pandemic year, but after vaccination, my body and mind breathed a sigh of relief, and I slept soundly through most nights. But as I thought about re-entering society (whatever that meant), I had several dreams and brought one into my therapy session.

I was returning from the Jersey Shore, taking a bus into Manhattan, along with my brother, John. But instead of going directly to Port Authority, the bus dropped us off in the woods in New Jersey in the middle of the night. There was no connection back to New York City until the next morning.

Looking for shelter, we found a funky depot that recalled the tiny Bay Head train station, but we left because crazy people were inside. We landed up crashing in a house. The owners were not home, and I worried we'd get busted. We were hungry and raided the refrigerator and sat at the kitchen table eating.

I was annoyed with my brother and blamed him for not knowing this bus didn't go into Manhattan. And I was angry at myself because I'd forgotten my phone and didn't have much money. I was unprepared, and we were stuck in limbo.

"Getting stranded in the woods in the middle of the night feels like a perfect analogy for my transition into post-pandemic life," I said, offering my interpretation in the session. "Eventually, a bus would come and take me home, but meanwhile, I'm stuck in this weird, uncomfortable situation."

"Why did you rely upon your brother to get the schedule instead of getting it yourself?" asked my therapist, whose questions were always sharp.

"Good question," I said. "Maybe I wanted someone else to take care of me."

I also mused about why my brother was on the bus with me. In real life, I commuted alone from the beach, and he drove me to or from the station. In the dream, I was glad I wasn't by myself in this scary situation.

"This year has been exhausting for you," interpreted my shrink. "You're alone and independent, and there's no one to take care of you. With your brother, you felt safe, and you had company, even though you were mad at him for messing up the bus schedule."

I reflected upon how the enforced solitude shaped me. It took away the advantages of living alone and underscored the negative parts of being single. The lockdowns would have been easier if I'd had a partner. Now that I was vaccinated, I had no excuse not to put more effort into finding a mate. After years of dating with no luck, I hadn't given up but had put dating on pause. I decided I was okay being alone and enjoyed my social life, hoping I might meet someone by going to everyday events. But then my carefully crafted social life blew up. Now I had a new perspective after spending so much time with no company. Having lived through the loneliness pandemic, I had to put myself out there again.

I thought about what I had lost this past year: I missed spending time and celebrating traditions with family and friends. I made a decision to leave my adjunct job teaching Personal Essay Writing at NYU. I loved teaching this class, but I didn't want to teach remotely, and it was too stressful not knowing what would happen in the future. So I retired a few years earlier than planned. I had just gotten my 30-year service award in the spring of 2020. I had a great run, yet I felt sad to give this up. My program director and colleagues said how much they'd miss me.

Fortunately, no one in my close circle of family or friends had died of Covid; two friends and two relatives who had gotten sick all recovered.

At the beginning of the epidemic, Dean, a former student of mine, died alone in his apartment in lower Manhattan. He didn't want to go to the hospital. A talented writer and actor, I helped him find his voice and get his first pieces published. I was upset when I heard the news. A gay man, Dean, survived the AIDS epidemic but died of Covid. A friend in New Jersey lost her mother in less than two weeks.

I read the notices on the "death board" in the mailroom. Two former tenants and two current Westbeth residents died of Covid. All were elderly. One woman, a playwright and publisher, wrote a farewell letter from her hospital room.

As the temperature hit the 60s, I started eating lunch outside at the Bus Stop Café. I wanted to support local businesses, and their lunch special was a good deal. I walked past the garden on Christopher Street where I'd buried tulip bulbs in the soil last fall. Many plants had popped up. They were a foot tall and ready to bud. A good omen.

Bridge and tunnel tourists were returning on the weekends. I think they missed the memo that "Real New Yorkers wear masks." I had loved the absence of tourists. When I visited the High Line during the winter, I could actually walk on it without zigzagging through the crowds. Europeans had packed the High Line, and tourism from outside the USA had fallen more than 80 percent.

At the annual spring meeting of the Westbeth Residents Council (on Zoom), the big questions were: When will the community room reopen? When will the gallery reopen? No dates were given. Westbeth was strictly following Covid protocols, which required many precautions for a public space. The room would have to be cleaned after every event, and the capacity would be less. It would be a totally different scene.

In the past, the community room was booked solid, with groups meeting back to back. If I arrived early for my singing workshop, the drawing class was winding down, putting away their sketchpads. As our chorus was belting out our last number, the projectionist came in to set up for the monthly movie night. Or a troupe of actors waited on the sidelines to start their rehearsal. Those halcyon days were over for now, but hopefully not forever.

The space was also rented for birthday parties and memorial services. Someone even had a wedding there. It was a neighborhood resource, not just for residents.

Looking back at March 2020, I was naive, trying to convince myself our group might resume inside in a few months. At my literary reading, the last hurrah before the lockdown, every chair was taken, and people were standing. I never imagined this valuable space would remain closed for regular events more than a year later. It was a huge loss.

Meanwhile, the large windows of the gallery and the community room that face the courtyard are being used for an anniversary exhibit, "Westbeth at 50." The show features huge, gorgeous photos of artists in their homes or studios (shot by Frankie Alduino for his book called *Vertical Village*).

Another exhibit in the Project Room, a small lobby, includes photos by *Life* magazine photojournalist Leonard Freed. An early resident, he shot the original tenants dancing in the courtyard, sculpting nude models, and smoking cigarettes in the gallery.

In the main hallway, an informative display—of text and photos—called "50 Creative Moments" tells an incredible history. Keith Haring had his first solo show at Westbeth, and the action star Vin Diesel grew up here. Early resident Muriel Rukeyser wrote a poem about the artists moving into their spaces. *Hedwig and the Angry Inch* was developed in the Westbeth Theater Center. An early hip-hop album featuring Busta Rhymes was produced in a basement studio by a group of young Westbeth residents. The list went on.

I was checking out this artistic legacy while waiting in the lobby for my grocery delivery. The maintenance staff was buzzing.

"Have you seen the pictures in the courtyard?" a porter asked as he mopped the floor.

"Yeah, they're great," I said.

"They're bringing the building back to life," said our assistant super.

I nodded in agreement, thinking what an honor to live here among all these great artists, past and present.

Whenever I walked past the giant photos of neighbors living and dead, I thought of the Joni Mitchell song "The Circle Game."

I decided to savor whatever I could. On a beautiful warm spring day, I sat in the courtyard reading Anne Lamott's new book *Dusk, Night, Dawn: On Revival and Courage*. I pulled down my mask and felt the sun on my face for the first time since last year.

The outer courtyard at Westbeth

My Life Needs a Refresh Button

APRIL 2021

This was my second pandemic Easter. My niece had invited me to an outdoor dinner with a smaller crowd than in the past. I debated what to do. I wanted to see my family. The last time I saw them was during the summer at the beach. I had not been to a holiday family get-together since Christmas 2019.

But it would mean taking the bus from Port Authority to suburban New Jersey. The bus is always crowded on a holiday, and I'd be sitting with a stranger in a double seat. And there's no way we could space out six feet in line on that stupid little platform where we waited for the bus. I kept getting mixed signals. The Centers for Disease Control said it was safe to travel if you were vaccinated. But they also said to keep all the precautions in place—masks and social distancing—but what if I couldn't do that on a packed bus to New Jersey?

Even though I wanted to start getting back into the world, this holiday trip did not seem like a good idea. When I went to the beach during the summer, I took the train at an off-hour, and the car was nearly empty. When I rode the bus in NYC, I got a solo seat, and my trip was short.

And I was tired. My shrink was right. I was exhausted after spending a year taking care of myself on my own. I'd never let up. I took precautions, made schedules, cleaned my apartment, did laundry, shopped for groceries, prepared good food, and exercised every day. That took a lot out of me.

Better to stay in the city this Easter and relax. My mood was more hopeful than last spring, but I flitted from hopeful to depressed. I was slowly coming out of this dark period of isolation. Before the pandemic, I was busy making post-retirement career plans. Now, my brain was so foggy that I could barely remember them.

After spending a long year obsessing about staying safe, I was burned out. I was even losing interest in doing yoga, which always made me feel good. An article in the *New York Times* called this a "late pandemic crisis of purpose." I totally related and wondered how I could muster the energy to pursue a social life again. I decided not to put pressure on myself.

Then, on April 4, I streamed the Easter service from Middle Collegiate Church, which featured the recorded version of the "Hallelujah" chorus from Easter Sunday two years ago. I was there. The whole congregation was standing and singing, rocking out to this jazzed up rendition, the closing hymn. No one could've ever believed this would be the last time we'd celebrate Easter inside that beautiful sanctuary. (I was still in shock that Middle Church had burned down last December.)

After watching the service and making a donation, I left Westbeth to go for a walk, and I saw a priest who'd just parked his car on Bank Street. He was wearing a black cassock and a Roman collar. My inner Catholic schoolgirl kicked in.

"Happy Easter, Father," I said.

"God bless you," he said and waved.

I felt glad I had stayed in the city. A priest had just blessed me, and I was headed to Washington Square Park to listen to live music—jazz and swing. I began to realize it would be a long time before things returned to normal. Or maybe we would be living in a new normal.

I had to recreate a social life in this emerging world. With that goal in mind, I attended a small meetup on Zoom, sponsored by the women's branch of Out Professionals. I even dressed up for the occasion. I put on a shirt with a collar instead of a T-shirt. After introductions, the organizer led a freewheeling discussion about how things had changed in the lesbian community over the years. The women seemed smart, well educated, and very aware. The meetup ended with the organizer describing the in-person activities she was planning.

This sounded like a portal to reentry. I had to start somewhere. I downloaded my Excelsior pass from a New York State website. I printed it out and took a picture with my phone. I planned to attend some events that would require proof of vaccination. New York was the first state to offer this digital proof.

In April, an editor tossed me an assignment from a website I wrote for before the pandemic. Work had slowed down for a year, but now it was coming back. I should have been enthusiastic, but I felt lethargic. Or was this the state called languishing? I had to pump myself up, even though I was glad to have the income. It would be good to write about subjects other than the virus. I had abandoned my mystery novel when we went into lockdown and never came back to it. It seemed frivolous.

I was in this weird transition. When my neighbor introduced me to her mother in the lobby, her mother put her hand out to shake. But I had already put my elbow out to bump, so I bumped her hand with my elbow. In my yoga class for seniors, the older folks were now giving advice to our teacher, Jen, about how to schedule the vaccine. She had just become eligible for people over 30. "Keep hitting refresh," one woman advised her.

I feel like my life needs a refresh button.

Kate's garden

Getting Back Out There

SPRING 2021

I started a campaign to refresh my life. I invited friends and neighbors and colleagues to see the exhibit "Westbeth at 50." I always wanted to be a tour guide, so this was my chance. But it was more than that. Giving tours became the gateway to reopening my life.

We met in the courtyard, and I guided my guests through the display of the giant photos as I talked a little about each artist. Then we went inside the lobby to view the other shows. I never took more than two visitors on my sightseeing trips, and we all wore masks.

I had fun, something that had been missing in my life. As I narrated the visit to my building, I appreciated how lucky I was to be living in Westbeth Artists Housing. I gave eight informal tours; friends popped over from the East Village and the West Village, even from New Jersey. Then we went to lunch or had a drink. People hugged me when they arrived and when they left. Hugs and company. This had not happened in a long time.

Two colleagues came down from the Upper West Side. I'd met Elizabeth and Beckie in a Zoom group for writers formed during the pandemic. Although we'd interacted for months, we'd never met in person and only seen each other from the waist up. They came to my apartment and we chatted for about half an hour. Then I took them on the tour and later we went for chai lattes.

Elizabeth seemed much more relaxed in person than on the Zoom calls. Beckie was skinnier than I'd imagined and she thought I'd be taller. (I'm 5'5".) It was a lovely afternoon. I felt like I was making new friends, an unexpected perk of Zooming.

When my friend Kathleen came in from Princeton, she peppered me with questions about the history of Westbeth. Later, she treated me to lunch at Meme on Hudson Street, and we discussed potential plans for the July 4th weekend in Ocean Grove. We'd met there many years ago when we stayed at the same guesthouse in this weird Victorian town.

We got to know each other when we took long boardwalk walks every morning after coffee. I loved walking and talking as the sun rose over the ocean. Retired from social work, Kathleen was a political activist and very smart. A few years older, she gave me good advice about planning for retirement. Like me, she grew up Irish-Catholic in a big city in New Jersey.

Last summer was the first time in over ten years that I'd missed spending the July 4th holiday in Ocean Grove. The place where we always stayed had been closed, but now it was reopened. But this B&B (like many of the century-old guesthouses) had shared bathrooms in the hall. That never bothered me before, but now it felt weird.

The more we talked, the more questions arose. Will staff and guests be wearing masks in the common areas? How will the B&B handle breakfast? That communal ritual of sitting around the dining table socializing with other guests after heaping my plate with food from the buffet was my favorite part of guesthouse life. Now this idea made me uncomfortable. Many holiday customs I took for granted now required major rethinking.

Kathleen told me she was finding it harder to adjust to post-vaccination life than to the lockdown. (At least back then, we all knew the rules.) She thought everyone was a little depressed. How could we not be?

After lunch, I took my friend on an improvised tour of the quaint winding streets of historic Greenwich Village. We walked along West 4th Street to Sheridan Square, then across Grove Street, back to Hudson.

"You live in such a beautiful neighborhood," she observed as we strolled past a cherry tree in bloom.

We finished with a rest stop in the Gardens of St. Luke in the Fields. Spring was magnificent this year. The azaleas were dazzling. The tulips looked bigger and brighter. Was it because it snowed this past winter? (That's supposed to be good for bulbs.) Or maybe my perception was different as my state of mind improved. Last spring, as I rushed in and out during the lockdown, I was too freaked out to appreciate the flowers.

My improvised tours were a hit. I got rave reviews:

"We enjoyed ourselves tremendously."

"Nice to see Westbeth and your West Village."

"I'm giving your tour five stars."

I went by myself to the Westbeth Gallery but not to see art. I was donating blood again, a civic gesture I'd started doing during the pandemic. It was an easy way to help my fellow New Yorkers. And I had an uncommon blood type that was in demand: B negative. Setting up the blood bank in the gallery was a creative reuse of our community space.

But I had flashbacks. Donors checked in at the desk where, in the past, I signed the guestbook for the artist's show. I was directed to a computer to answer questions and then had vital signs taken. My temperature and blood pressure were normal, and my iron was good. All set.

As I lay there in a reclining chair, watching my blood go into the bag, I recalled the many good times at various openings. The chairs for donors were set up near the area where our resident bartender once served wine and soda. I felt a little sad when I looked at the empty walls and hoped the gallery would reopen in the fall.

The drinks and snacks were on tables in a side gallery. Now I had a good excuse to eat a bag of potato chips and some pretzels since it was recommended you have a salty snack after giving blood. As I rested in the snack area, I chatted with a young woman who used to take classes at the Martha Graham studio on the top floor of Westbeth. Now her classes were on Zoom.

I'm fortunate to live a few blocks from the Whitney Museum, now located in the trendy Meatpacking District. I made reservations and saw two fabulous shows. The large abstract paintings by Julie Mehretu radiated energy. The black and white portraits by the street photographer Dawoud Bey knocked me out.

In a weird twist of "only in New York," a few days before I went to the museum, I was walking through the streets of Chelsea and saw an older Black man carrying a gigantic camera. I had a hunch it was the photographer whose show I was planning to see. When I got home, I Googled and found a documentary about Bey. I was right. The museum guard said the artist often came in to check out his show. He was probably headed there when I saw him.

I was happy to get my sidewalk garden going again. I loved this annual ritual. I was an avid urban gardener who had tended a box outside my building for over 15 years. My two hydrangeas had leaves. The ivy had new sprouts. Time to start planting the annuals. Every spring, I selected flowering plants and created a design in my sidewalk box.

I learned from past experience what worked well in this location. I favored begonias, impatiens, verbena, dianthus, and geraniums for color; dusty miller for borders, sweet potato vines to drape over the side. I kept notes of what I planted each year. I basked in compliments from grateful neighbors.

Buying colorful annuals required numerous trips on the 14th Street crosstown bus to the Union Square Greenmarket. Last spring, when I made these runs (and the city was still in lockdown), I was scared to take the bus and limited my trips. The bus was free, and the driver sat behind a plastic curtain. I walked to the market, but I rode back because the plants weighed a lot. Even though I wore gloves on my short trips, I worried I'd get Covid from touching the doors, the poles, the buzzer. But I enjoyed gardening so much that it was worth the risk.

This April, I was not anxious because I knew Covid was not spread by touching things. And I was vaccinated. What a difference a year made.

Finally, the CDC said that those vaccinated did not need to wear masks outdoors unless in a crowded situation. Truthfully, I didn't see much change in the appearance of pedestrians on the busy sidewalks of Manhattan in the days after this announcement. Almost everyone was still masked. But I did start to wear my mask below my nose if no one was around.

Marijuana legalization had recently passed in New York State, and on April 20, members of ACT-UP and other activists handed out free joints in Union Square Park to those who could prove they were fully vaccinated. I liked the idea of connecting the two.

By the end of the month, anyone could get a vaccine by walking into a site. What a contrast from the winter when I hustled to get an appointment when my age group became eligible.

This coming June, I planned to attend the Queer Liberation March, which I missed last year out of concern for my health. I wondered if groups would be marching to advocate vaccination. New themes emerged every year based upon current events.

Then I found a box on the sidewalk with the *Village Voice*. The legendary weekly had shut down completely in 2018; now it was back in print as a quarterly. As I took a copy of this new edition from the blue box, I recalled how excited I was when I finally got a byline in the music section in the 1980s. I felt like I had arrived as a New York writer. Every time I had a piece in there, I raced out to grab several copies.

As I opened the familiar paper on the bus, I started reading their current "worst landlord" story—a classic *Village Voice* feature that would never lack material. Peter Noel's piece from the archives "Driving While Black" from 1998 could have been written today. An article on the return of live music took me forward. And of course, there was a feature about moving beyond this last unbelievable year. The next day, I found stacks of the paper in my lobby.

The rebirth of the iconic *Village Voice* felt like a positive sign. The headline on the front page of the spring 2021 issue said, "New York's coming back. And so are we."

At the end of April, I had lunch outside at La Bonbonniere, an old-school diner with a fancy name. This place had been around a long time. A few years ago, they filmed a segment of *The Marvelous Mrs. Maisel* inside because the décor looked like the '50s.

I usually had lunch at the Bus Stop Café, but I wanted to support another local diner. I knew La Bonbonniere had barely survived the pandemic. Their not accepting credit cards did not help the situation.

I was sitting at a table set up on the sidewalk; it wasn't a formal sidewalk café. My chair was bumping against a delivery bike locked to a street sign. My waitress, an older Latina woman, maybe late fifties, was very friendly as I asked about the inexpensive lunch menu.I ordered a coke and an eggplant parmigiana sandwich (which was really good). Later, when she gave me the check, she told me she'd worked there for 30 years.

While I waited for my food, I overheard her talking to a couple who walked past. They obviously knew each other and the couple was happy to run into the chatty server. My ears perked up when I listened to this conversation.

"I got the vaccine," said the waitress, all excited. "I got the Pfizer, and I feel young. It made me feel like a tiger."

The couple started laughing, and the woman said, "You were always a tiger."

The waitress replied, "But now I'm a young tiger."

Now I was laughing too. I loved this idea of the vaccine as the Fountain of Youth. She told the couple she got the vaccine in that new place, the one that used to be St. Vincent's Hospital. (She was referring to Northwell Health, on Seventh Avenue, housed in one of the old St. Vincent's buildings. The rest was turned into condos.)

As she mentioned the vaccination site, I remembered going to Northwell last spring at seven o'clock during the height of the pandemic, standing outside with my neighbors and cheering the health care workers. I also recalled walking past the refrigerated trucks on the side street next to the small hospital across from the AIDS memorial. This was the second plague I had lived through in New York City.

I Know I've Been Changed

MAY 2021

As the month of May rolled on, more of New York was opening up. As if the pandemic was over. But was it? Yes, Covid cases and hospitalizations were down. More New Yorkers were getting vaccinated daily, but we were nowhere near herd immunity.

According to the governor's daily email on May 14, only 51 percent of New Yorkers were fully vaccinated, while 61 percent had gotten one shot. The decisions felt rushed. Like a gamble. I was apprehensive about this sudden shift after being careful for 15 months.

Over a year ago, New York City shut down when the virus spread with fast speed, but now the city was picking up speed as the virus slowed down. My emotions bounced around. I was rooting for the comeback but wondered if this was too soon. Only time would tell. I decided to trust my judgment and remain very careful. This stage was now all about individual decision-making and personal comfort level. Going to an outdoor concert worked for me, especially if we could sit apart, but I couldn't picture myself attending a Broadway show at full capacity.

"Everyone has a different idea of what's safe," said Dr. R. "And there's a whole range of in-between. But it's very exciting to do all these things we took for granted."

I had taught Critical Thinking for ten years at the community college. As New York City and the country reopened, my critical thinking skills would be put to good use on a regular basis as I made decisions about traveling and attending events.

I was shocked when the CDC stated that fully vaccinated people no longer needed to wear masks indoors in most situations and no longer needed to physically distance. When this announcement was made in the middle of May, only 35 percent of the general population was fully vaccinated. Sixty percent of Americans had at least one dose.

The big problem was how did we know? We were now on the honor system. I trusted people I knew but not strangers. The *Washington Post* columnist Dr. Leana S. Wen, who specializes in public health, wrote an opinion piece titled, "The CDC Shouldn't Have Removed Restrictions Without Requiring Proof of Vaccination." I agreed and worried how this might play out.

As more restrictions were dropped, I realized that coming back to life wasn't as simple as contacting friends and going to lunch. Or making reservations for a museum date. During the past long year, I'd been profoundly rocked by loneliness and anxiety and a sense of my mortality. I still had the article I had clipped, "My Coronavirus Will." I thought about what my therapist had said recently, "The entire pandemic is about loss and sadness."

The pandemic was extra hard for people like me who are single and live alone. I had no partner and no pod. I suffered from "skin hunger," a state of longing that results from touch deprivation. As I scheduled a massage, I knew I'd never take touch for granted again. As I reconnected with friends and colleagues, in-person conversations came back into my life. I had missed that. I was delighted when my (vaccinated) guests sat on my couch, without masks, and we talked. This simple activity filled me with joy.

I am not the same person who had celebrated the holidays with family and friends and neighbors in December 2019. Shortly after that festive period, I spent a year isolated with very little in-person contact. My old life had been erased.

I'm not sure what comes next. But it must include fun and pleasure and people who get me. And live music and book events, and singing and dancing, and swimming in the ocean. I planned to return to the family beach bungalow earlier this year.

After what I'd gone through, I was determined to live and love again. I'll only hang out with people who replenish me and make me feel connected, and I'll only do work that gives me joy. I'll pull back from people addicted to drama. Life is too short for stressful assignments or draining people.

I started making up for lost time, doing lots of activities. I had an amazing hour-long massage from Noelle, whose office is off Union Square Park. (The last time I saw her was January 2020.) I felt great when I left. The massage was almost better than sex.

It was a stunning spring day, 72 degrees, blue skies with few clouds. As I walked toward 14th Street past the vendors that ring the Greenmarket, I heard the Alicia Keys song "If I Ain't Got You." It was so loud that I thought it was coming from a car stereo. But then I looked around and saw a singer. An Asian woman with dyed blond hair wearing chunky high-heeled shoes. Her phone was hooked up to a speaker. She was super emotional as she belted out the signature line, "Some people want diamond rings."

As I waited for the light to change, the woman standing next to me said, "Sing it, girl."

What a perfect New York moment. On the corner of University Place, a gifted street singer was nailing a great song by Alicia Keys (a quintessential New Yorker who grew up in Hell's Kitchen). I went over and threw money into the box.

My Westbeth neighbor and friend, SuZen, invited me to her birthday party, a sunset soiree on the pier in Hudson River Park. It was a big birthday. She was 75 on May 17.

SuZen is a fantastic photographer and multimedia artist who has exhibited widely. A practicing Buddhist, she always seems upbeat and has the energy of a younger person. When we were both still teaching, we often met in the elevator in the morning on our way to work.

This was the first party I'd attended in over a year. Ironically, one of the last parties I'd attended before the lockdown was in December 2019 at SuZen's apartment down the hall. So this really felt like coming full circle. In May 2021, we would party like it was 2019.

When I got to the end of the pier, I added my chocolate cookies from the bakery to a picnic table filled with chips and dips and crudites and sushi and wine and seltzer. As people kept arriving, I introduced myself or said hello. Some guests were neighbors I already knew from my building. Others I'd met at previous parties. And some new faces. A woman brought a beautiful birthday cake she custom ordered from the Magnolia Bakery. We admired it as she opened the box.

We danced, we drank, we sang. We took pictures along the railing of the pier with the sun setting in the background. We listened to The Beatles, Van Morrison, Bob Marley. I wondered what the young people at the nearby tables thought about this boomer music.

At some point, we filled up our plastic flutes with champagne, and we toasted SuZen. She thanked us for coming. Just as we were finishing up with the champagne and cake, the park police arrived in a car, pulling right up to our table. Two officers jumped out. The male officer told us that drinking in the park was illegal (of course, we knew that). I told the officers we were celebrating a big birthday.

They were very friendly, and the female officer told us to get rid of the bottles. So we swept the empties into the recycling can and put the others away into a backpack. We were lucky the police were so good-natured. We could've been fined. Did they let us slide because we're old? Or because they knew we'd been cooped up for over a year? Or both?

"We got busted," I joked after they left. "Now, it's really a party." The idea of the cops busting a group of senior citizens was pretty funny. Earlier, I'd heard two people discussing Medicare advantage plans.

I walked back to Westbeth with a neighbor as the party started to break up. I was carrying two bowls and two trays that I would return to SuZen the next day. My neighbor, a sculptor, said it was the first time he'd been in a crowd (I'd counted about 20 people) in over a year.

"Me too," I said, as we both agreed it was a great evening. And the weather had really cooperated.

As we approached our building, my neighbor realized he'd lost his mask during the revelry. I usually carry an extra but didn't have one that night. I put mine on as we entered the side door through the courtyard. He went to the desk and apologized for not having a mask (still required inside our building.) I think the security guards had extras. He was at the desk talking when I went into the elevator, my arms full of party supplies.

This evening was a turning point. I felt happy and liberated as I entered my apartment. That same week, I saw a sign in the elevator that the Westbeth community room was reopening (with restrictions) on June 1. That was great news. And then I found out the gallery was reopening in September.

On June 1, I attended staff appreciation day in the Westbeth courtyard. Residents turned out in large numbers to cheer the incredible workers who kept us safe during the pandemic. They got a standing ovation and received a well-deserved bonus from the Residents Council.

After the ceremony, I went to the New York Public Library on Hudson Street to pick up a book I'd reserved. My branch was now open for brief browsing. I spent a glorious 20 minutes looking through the shelves.

"I'm so happy I can browse again," I said to the librarian as I checked out two books.

"It's wonderful," she replied.

During the month of May, as I walked around the reawakening city, this gospel song I knew from Middle Church kept running through my head, "I Know I've Been Changed." I listened to different versions. Loved the one by the Staple Singers, slow and bluesy.

No wonder this soulful spiritual kept looping in my mind. It is about faith and redemption and transformation, about crossing the river to the other side. I had made it over.

Poster on Washington Street, August 2020

Postscript

When I sent this book to my publisher in the middle of June 2021, Covid was in retreat in the USA—thanks to those citizens who masked up and got the vaccine. And thanks to local and federal government that managed the rollout with care and competence. At this point, about 60 percent of all adults in the USA had received at least one dose, but the rate varied greatly from state to state

As of June 15, New York State reached a vaccination goal: 70 percent of adult New Yorkers had received at least one dose of the Covid vaccine. As a result, Governor Cuomo lifted most of the state's remaining Covid restrictions. Fireworks lit the skies of the Empire state and New York launched an ad campaign: "Reimagine, Rebuild, Renew."

In New York City, during the course of the pandemic, 33,000 people died and 630,000 jobs were lost. Many residents fled to other locations. The new mayor (to be elected in November) faces a huge job ahead to revive our great city. The pandemic brought new problems and intensified existing ones, especially homelessness.

For months, cases declined as people got vaccinated. But then, as the summer wore on, as this book went through the editing process, there was a big shift. Just when it seemed safe to go back into the water or back into the supermarket without a mask, vaccination rates dropped—and the more contagious Delta variant swept in like a tornado. Numbers began to rise again with almost all the new cases coming from the Delta variant. And almost everyone getting sick and dying are unvaccinated.

What would it take to wake people up? How many more people would cry on their deathbed that they wish they had gotten vaccinated? How many more kids would lose their parents because they were afraid of the side effects of the vaccination? Thanks to the Delta variant, we've even had breakthrough infections among the people who are vaccinated, although the cases are much less severe.

I'm grateful to live in New York and vacation in New Jersey, two democratic states ruled by science. I feel badly for my friends who live in Florida. We really do live in two countries—divided into the red and the blue states. I'm proud of the leadership Governor Murphy showed in my native state. I'm glad he mandated masks in schools for this coming year. This will protect my two nieces who teach in New Jersey and their kids who are students.

I will always be a Jersey girl at heart even though I've lived in New York much longer. Sadly, Governor Cuomo will leave office in disgrace after showing strong leadership during the pandemic.

When I returned to Manhattan in the beginning of August, after spending three weeks at the Jersey Shore, I went grocery shopping. I put on a mask as I entered the supermarket and noticed almost everyone else in the store was also wearing a mask, a change from before I'd gone away on vacation. Things in New York City are still much improved than a year ago (pre-vaccine), but we've definitely lost ground. The sense of relief that I felt last May has faded, but I'm determined not to succumb to the fear I felt before I got the lifesaving jab.

I'm angry because it didn't have to be this way. I blame this regression on the folks who refuse to wear masks and refuse to get vaccinated. In my building, residents and visitors must still wear masks in all the common areas and abide by the two in an elevator rule. We do this as a community to protect each other.

When will this pandemic finally end? Will it ever?

Pandemic Writing Prompts

Writing helped me cope with anxiety, and I felt it was important to record what was going on during this unprecedented time. Now it's your turn to journal about your experiences during the pandemic. Here are some prompts to use as some jumping-off points.

1.) What was your last regular activity or last fun event before going into lockdown mode?

2.) Who or what did you miss most when your life shifted and became more restricted? Family? Friends? Classmates? Travel? Going to the local pub?

3.) What did you substitute for the activities you were missing? Did you take up a new pursuit or a hobby? Did your life move onto Zoom?

4.) How did you celebrate the holidays during the pandemic? Were you separated from family? Did you create new rituals?

5.) Did you have a point during the pandemic where you lost it or "hit a wall"? If so, when was this, and what happened?

6.) What was your experience with getting vaccinated? Were you anxious? Eager? Was it hard to schedule an appointment? How did you feel after being fully vaccinated?

7.) What activities made you feel like your life was getting back to normal? When was this? Did you eat inside a restaurant? Attend an event? Hug your grandkids?

8.) Were there any aspects of the pandemic lifestyle that you liked and will miss? Not having to commute in traffic every day? Not having to dress for work?

9.) Who do you consider the heroes of the pandemic? Health care workers? Grocery store employees? Delivery people? Your building staff?

10.) Who or what do you appreciate more now? What lessons did you learn from the pandemic?

11.) Did living through this extraordinary experience change your outlook on life? If so, how? Do you plan to make any changes in your lifestyle?

12.) Can you pick five words to describe your pandemic experience?

NOTES:

Like many people, I was preoccupied by staying safe from the coronavirus for over a year. As a journalist and essayist, the pandemic became the focus of my writing and resulted in *Behind the Mask*. As I wrapped up this book, I thought it was important to recall that I had a life before the coronavirus arrived here, and I wrote about many other things. I wanted to share that part of my life too. With that in mind, here are several of my favorite essays created in the years right before the pandemic.

PART TWO:
Life Before the Pandemic

Cleaning Out a Century of Family Life

WINTER AND SPRING 2018

I dreaded returning to Paterson, New Jersey, to clean out my child-hood home. Not only was it upsetting to see young men boldly smoking weed on the sidewalk in front of our porch, but the old house was packed with a century of family life. Fine china, collectibles, historical memorabilia, vintage books, and stylish clothes mingled with lots of junk.

My father was a packrat, and the three-family house had been in our tribe since 1903. It contained items from my grandparents as well as my parents, even things from my aunt and uncle. My father lived in this house for his entire 81 years. My mother moved in when they married, and she was still living there part-time when she died at 95. Sorting things out after our mom passed away was bound to be a time-consuming, emotional job.

During the six months we spent cleaning, my two siblings and I es-tablished a routine. We'd get there around ten in the morning, work for four or five hours with a half-hour lunch break at noon. We sat around the cluttered kitchen table eating the sandwiches my sister brought, or we heated up a frozen pizza. While we celebrated holidays together, there was always a big crowd around the table—spouses, kids, grand-kids, nieces, nephews. This was a chance for the three of us to spend time together.

I was the outsider middle child who always had the rockiest relation-ship with my parents. My older sister was the star child, scholarship win-ner, and best friends with my mother. My younger brother was the baby and only boy, "the little prince" who could do no wrong. Both my sib-lings lived in suburban New Jersey. They were retired teachers, married with children. I was gay, single, child-free, living in Greenwich Village.

Eating lunch together gave us the opportunity to bond. My brother mentioned his reading matter: the *Huffington Post*, *Daily Beast*, *New York Times*, and *Washington Post*. I didn't realize he was so interested in politics. Unlike our mother, he wasn't a Hillary fan, but he voted for her anyway. All three of us hated Trump.

We reminisced about local history. When my sister and I discussed the Paterson riots, we got into a disagreement because her story was different from mine. Then I realized we were talking about two separate sets. She was talking about the riots in the '60s, and I was talking about the riots in the '70s.

Our lunch break sometimes turned into a meeting about the estate. What other decisions needed to be made? I was amazed we got along so well during this draining job. No arguments or major disagreements. I'd read stories about siblings fighting over objects, but that didn't happen. Maybe when there is so much stuff, everyone walks away with items they want.

My therapist noted my parents had worked hard to create strong family bonds. The nuns once said we had the "model Catholic family." I was a rebel and a hippie who fought with my parents growing up, and they were confused when I came out as gay, but they did a good job creating unity among their three kids.

Many years ago, my mother had declared my brother should inherit my father's roll-top desk that was stored in the cellar. My grandmother bought it for my father when he started college. I always wanted it and felt it should be mine since I'm the writer in the family, but Mom thought it should go to her only son.

This was still unresolved when Mom died, but my brother told me I could have it. I thanked him, but since I had no space for it in my small Manhattan loft, the desk reverted back to him. But as it turned out, the desk had been ruined by coal dust and flooding. So we left it behind.

My friends didn't understand what it's like to clean out a house that's over 100 years old. They offered to stop by and take me to lunch. I declined. I was wearing ratty old jeans, and when I washed my hands for a lunch break, the water turned black. There was so much dust on shelves that had not been touched in years. My shrink called my parents closet hoarders.

Some days I resented that my parents had never made any major attempts to clean out this house. I figured they didn't take on this task because it was so overwhelming. I was burned out the day I tackled a cabinet filled with boxes of carbon paper, mimeograph paper, old lesson plans. My father retired in 1984, and he'd been dead for almost 20 years. I couldn't understand why he saved junk like boxes of carbon paper. On each visit, we usually hauled out ten to 12 giant hefty bags of stuff. I lost five pounds from running up and down the stairs from the second floor. I also hurt my back.

When we reached the attic storage room, my brother declared happily, "I'm finally going to finally get Dad's old Lionel trains. I've waited years for this."

My brother wanted them as a child and then later when his son was born (my nephew was now 37). My mother always said, "No, you can't get them. They're way in the back of the attic with too much stuff in front of them. Too much hassle. It would take days."

Now we were finally taking out all the boxes, and Mom was right. It took days to empty out this room and get to the trains. We found an erector set that belonged to my father as a boy and boxes of Tinkertoys, like the predecessor of Lego.

The day my brother cleaned out the tool closet, I made jokes about role-playing, but he knew about tools, and we didn't. We all pitched in as we emptied out the kitchen closet and the china cabinets. I felt sad when we wrapped up the good dishes we used on holidays and birthdays. I got a set, and so did my niece. We each took whatever decorative items we wanted, including vases that belonged to my grandmother and sat on the mantlepieces for as long as I could remember.

We uncovered family history. I found a cover letter that my father wrote when he was seeking a job in the public schools. I had no idea that my father, an English teacher, was also certified to teach Latin and math. I also found his little appointment book where my father, a sax player in a swing band, wrote down his gigs. On Valentine's Day in 1948, he had a job at the Packanack Lake clubhouse, where we held my mother's surprise 90th birthday party years later.

I found a diary that my grandfather, Will Walter, kept in 1899. He commuted by the Erie Railroad to a job in Manhattan as a lithographer. He was 23 and dating my grandmother, Annie. I had never met my grandparents, but now they were coming to life. Will walked Annie home from church and took her to the opera. I inherited the beautiful opera glasses they used.

It was challenging to figure out what to do with valuable things but getting collectibles to the right folks was more important than getting money. We gave items to select people who would cherish them: old playbills, *Life* magazines, baseball memorabilia, and sheet music went to family and friends. A local historian with a website came to the house and scanned in memorabilia related to Paterson before we gave the box to the historical society.

Various family members got the old Victrola, the china cabinet, the dining room table, and a chiffarobe. I schlepped clothes to a hip vintage consignment shop in the East Village and kept a small bookcase and vintage books inscribed by my father and grandfather.

It was a relief that the upstairs tenant, who was buying the house, said we could leave whatever furniture we didn't want, and then she could rent that floor semi-furnished. We told her to take all the clothes left in the closets because she's petite like my mother, and they were close. It took half a year to clean out over 100 years of family life. We started in January and finished in June when the movers came to take the furniture pieces we wanted. As the months passed, I realized our weekly routine was like a healing balm, a cleansing. We were orphan siblings working through our grief as we sorted through family objects.

Saving the Memory of Old New York

SPRING 2018

As I walked into Cobblestones, a vintage shop in the East Village, I heard swing music, the kind my dad played in a band in the 1940s. Ceiling fans were spinning above the long, narrow space packed with purses, shoes, hats, dresses, blouses. The owner, Delanee Koppersmith, sat at a cluttered desk with a rotary dial phone. The store had no cash register.

I'd been sad as I cleaned out my childhood home in Paterson, New Jersey after my widowed mother died. My deceased parents never threw anything out, and now we were selling the house. But I felt rejuvenated when Koppersmith, 59, loved my mother's scarves and gushed over my father's ties—wide, skinny, silk, hand-painted. She said some were rare.

My dad was a sharp dresser and always wore a tie to work. I brought her dozens. As the vintage dealer went through my stash, she pulled out a gorgeous blue number and said, "It's so beautiful. You should keep this for yourself and wear it." So I kept it. She put the ties on display, selling for $28 to $36.

I even brought in my own stuff. The white fur stole I wore to the junior prom landed up in the shop window. I also gave her a plaid spring coat, very Jackie Kennedy. When Koppersmith checked out the pockets, she handed me a pair of rosary beads. One day, while I was in the store, a young woman bought my mother's pretty blue scarf for $12. Koppersmith winked at me. I felt this sale was a sign from my mother. Mom was saying hello, no doubt pleased someone appreciated her stylishness.

Each time I left with an itemized receipt with an estimate of what the store would charge for each item. I'd get half when it sold. I had no idea how Koppersmith could keep track of who gave her what. There was always a pile of new acquisitions on the floor. But I knew she did a good job remembering.

My fashionable ex-girlfriend used to bring in items she found at yard sales Upstate. That was how I first met the owner. I called her when going through my parents' clothes. I started babbling about the great stuff. Koppersmith offered condolences.

As I started swinging by, I learned her routine for running a small business that had survived for decades. The store was open six days a week from 1:00 until 8:00. I figured she was able to relax at home in the mornings. But Koppersmith told me she got up at 6:00 every day and was in the shop by 9:00 dusting, straightening, arranging. She mentioned taking things home to clean and press.

"Did you ever consider getting an intern?" I asked. "Like a student from FIT?"

"Many people have volunteered to help," she said. "But it's better for me to be in charge."

Tall and thin, with big, dark hair, Koppersmith often wore tuxedo pants, a ruffled blouse, and a jaunty neckerchief. She grew up on the Lower East Side and has owned Cobblestones on East Ninth Street for 37 years. She moved to her current location, between First and Second Avenues, in 1989. She called the block "the Madison Avenue of the East Village." In its heyday, there were more than 30 venues, "interesting stores with character," she noted. I was impressed her shop had lasted so long.

"Lots of things explain my success," she said. "I have a good variety, and I've always kept my hours. I've worked hard, and I've been lucky. I love the clothes I sell. My favorite periods are the '30s and '40s. The graphic designs were so beautiful then. Just look at the boxes. It was a calmer, simpler time when family meant everything, and life was valued."

I asked how she'd come by her affinity for the past. "I definitely think I lived in the '40s," she said. "I died young, and I returned. Now I'm collecting the belongings I had back then.

"People come in for costumes for plays," she said. "Designers of shoes and textiles come in for inspiration. The neighborhood used to have more musicians and artists when the rents were cheap. Now they are in Brooklyn. Business is not what it used to be. Internet sales have really hurt, as well as the buy-and-trade outlets."

While I emptied out drawers and closets in my parents' house, making many trips into Cobblestones, I got an idea of what sold. I showed her iPhone photographs of bags and blouses and dresses, and I'd only retrieve what the shopkeeper wanted. She rejected some of Mom's clothes as "too mature" for her young customers. Since it was spring, she didn't need winter apparel. But she advised which cold-weather items to hold for her—a fur wrap, a muffler.

As I dropped off items weekly, it was as if my parents came back to life through their clothes and accessories.

"Your father was really thin," Koppersmith commented as she tried on the black tuxedo jacket he wore as a sax player in a swing band. "Someone will buy this for a play."

"Yes, he was thin and tall," I said, showing her a photo of my father wearing it.

"Oh, my God, he was so handsome," she remarked. "What color eyes did he have?"

"Blue," I said. (Mine are brown like my mother's.)

When I brought in two pairs of Mom's shoes, Koppersmith said, "What a tiny foot."

I told her my mother was only five feet tall, very petite, and weighed 90 to 100 pounds most of her life. I never realized her foot was that small. One was a pair of pointy-toed mesh high heels that my mother dyed gold to wear to a formal dinner; the other was a gorgeous pair of black velvet flats with colorful sequins.

"Well, that's interesting," she said. "Your mom was short, and your dad was tall. I bet the tall women were really jealous that she landed a tall guy when a short woman like her could've ended up with a short guy."

I never viewed my parents' height status that way. It seemed the shopkeeper was thinking the way people thought back in the 1940s when my folks married. This woman was totally into the past. As I uncovered stacks of Broadway Playbills when I cleaned out the house, I liked the idea of an actor sporting my father's tux on stage.

Koppersmith has an upbeat personality, greeting each customer who walks into the shop.

"Hello, young lady," she'll say. "How is your afternoon going? Let me know if I can help you with anything."

What got this woman interested in this quirky occupation? I asked as she rummaged through a bag of goodies I'd brought in for her appraisal.

"I didn't go to college," Koppersmith said. "I worked for a designer and then briefly moved to Arizona. When I came back, I was 21 and thought, what am I going to do with my life? By then, things started gentrifying in the East Village. My mother always talked about having a vintage store, but she had a job with benefits, so it was up to me. When I initially opened in 1981, my rent was $450 a month. I painted the walls, put up shelves. In the first store, I had more glassware and jewelry and less clothing."

I recalled her first place since I had moved from New Jersey to the East Village in 1975 and lived in the neighborhood for two decades. As a witness to the gentrification, I was curious if her clientele had changed.

"My customers are mainly young women, students, and locals," Koppersmith said. "I also get a lot of tourists, especially in the summer. I can sit in my chair and go around the world.

"Another thing I love about running this business," she added, "is that I take things on consignment from senior citizens. They are thrilled that their possessions have another life, and the income helps them. Through my store, I'm saving the memory of old New York."

Cobblestones, a vintage shop on East 9th Street, October 2021

Signing a Legacy

OCTOBER 2018

I wondered if I was crazy to be taking the train from Penn Station to Bay Head that Friday when a Nor'easter was predicted for the Jersey Shore, but this year was the 20th anniversary of Bonnie's sunrise brunch. I'd already committed to attending. Bonnie was my neighbor in Ocean Beach and my favorite yoga teacher. When I took her beach class during the summer, we paused if dolphins swam past. I felt obligated to attend this event in memory of my mother, who never missed it.

This end-of-season tradition took place every October. When the weather was good, people gathered around a driftwood bonfire to watch the sunrise and take photos.

I knew there wouldn't be a sunrise this time. But there would still be a sumptuous brunch at Claire's house. Bonnie and Claire were close friends, new-age types, and year-round dwellers on Barnegat Island. Claire's spacious house had a great layout for a crowd: a big living room and a sun porch off the kitchen.

I hadn't gone to this party in ages due to my work schedule, but now I was retired and missed the banter of my colleagues. This year, with the Nor'easter, the weather reminded me of the time I attended with my mom, who was propping me up through a bad breakup. It was very stormy that weekend too, with no sunrise. Except now I was here alone.

The summer after my lesbian partner dumped me after 26 years, I retreated to the beach house to get comforted by my Irish Catholic mother, who totally got it. "It's just like getting a divorce," she said, worried about my emotional state.

When I'd first come out decades ago, my parents were not happy, but Mom had become more open and accepting after my father died. She told me that reading helped her get through Dad's death. So we read, sitting together on the beach with our novels or curled into our favorite chairs at night. That fall, we went to this same party in a storm, so this weekend felt like Deja vu.

On Saturday morning, I put on a rain jacket and walked out of our bungalow into 60 mph wind. Garbage cans were rolling across the road. Chairs were knocked over. I cut across a yard and dashed up the next street to my neighbor's house. Bonnie and Claire were delighted to see me and introduced me to people I didn't know.

As a child and teenager, I loved spending summers in Ocean Beach, yet as an adult, I felt a bit estranged from the neighbors. Most were married with kids and grandkids and lived in suburban New Jersey. I was the gay writer from Greenwich Village.

While I settled on the sofa with a plate of scrambled eggs and fruit salad, I spied the guestbook for the annual sunrise brunch. I flipped back to 2017, the year my mother died. Someone wrote, "We miss you, Agnes, and your lemon poppyseed coffee cake." I got choked up.

I knew Mom always baked a loaf cake, but I didn't remember what kind. This year, I'd wanted to bring something authentic from New York City that they couldn't easily find at the Jersey Shore. I'd bought rugelach from a Jewish bakery on Second Avenue. The pastries went fast. Everyone loved them, declaring the real thing much better than the Walmart version.

I flashed back to another time I was at this party, when I was 57, sitting in the living room with a group of older women, my mother's friends, in their 80s and 90s. Mom said, "Why don't you go sit on the porch with all the young people?" To her, I was still young then.

I enjoyed chatting with Claire's mother, who remembered me as a kid. She said she felt ancient hearing the Ocean Beach residents she knew as children were now retired. She and my mother used to attend Bonnie's chair yoga class for seniors. With my mother gone, Claire's mother was the only one left from that first generation of homeowners who settled here in the 1950s. Now my brother and sister and I were the owners of my parents' beach bungalow.

Feeling nostalgic, I flipped further into the guestbook. I found my mother's signature and her comment in her small, pinched handwriting: "I had a wonderful time." I saw the names of other women from her generation who had passed, including her friend who coincidentally died on the same date, July 26, but years earlier. Both widows, they used to take day trips to Atlantic City together to have dinner and play the slot machines.

I was glad the visitor log had survived Superstorm Sandy, which had devastated our barrier island. The book must have been stored on Bonnie's second floor because her first floor was underwater.

As I signed my name on the page for 2018, I remembered that I used to think these books were corny. But now I realized their value. The guest list became a tribute to my mother and our neighbors who built this community. I raised my coffee cup in their memory.

Bedroom at the Walter Family Bunglalow, Ocean Beach, NJ

Woodstock: My Queer Love Story

AUGUST 2019

"Want to go to Woodstock with me?" my boyfriend Joe asked.

"Yes!" I screamed at his offer. I was a 20-year-old student at a conservative Catholic women's college in New Jersey. Joe was my guide into the radical '60s.

We'd met at the Jersey Shore when my sorority rented a house in Belmar, a party town. Joe was four years older than me, already out of school. He had a job, his own apartment, a motorcycle, and long hair. My father disliked him. It didn't help when my mother found my birth control pills in my dresser.

Joe was over six feet tall, with black hair and dark eyes, kinda hairy and a bit chubby, a bear—not my type at all. He had wire-rimmed glasses, like his idol, John Lennon, and wore vests with fringe. Since Joe was the music editor for *The Aquarian*, a popular underground newspaper, we became regulars at the Fillmore East. Nothing could have kept us two rockers from the three-day music festival in the lower Catskills.

That was so long ago; Joe and I were both still straight. Years later, in the '70s, we came out—first him, then me. (No wonder the sex wasn't so hot.)

I'll never forget how early Thursday morning, August 14, 1969, Joe picked me up at the Jersey Shore. Then we drove to East Brunswick to connect with his brother and his brother's girlfriend. They followed us in their car.

Joe drove his black Karmann Ghia convertible, a two-seater with a tiny trunk. The tents and backpacks with sleeping bags were in the bigger car in our little caravan upstate. Joe's Italian mother, a great cook, packed enough food in the cooler to last for days. Good thing, because the local stores and restaurants sold out. We never expected to be trapped on this big muddy field with roads blocked, and the Thruway shut down.

"Hippies Mired in a Sea of Mud," read the *Daily News* headline. No wonder my parents were worried.

When we arrived that evening, vehicles were lined up for miles along Route 17B, the road that led to the site in the town of White Lake. We ditched the two cars along the roadside, slipped on our backpacks, grabbed the cooler and tents, and followed the crowds to Yasgur's farm. No one asked for our tickets.

On Friday, we had plans to meet our friends, Terry and Leslie, who drove up separately. Terry had been drafted into the army, which meant going to Viet Nam. He was scheduled to leave that Monday.

As Joe and I trudged up a ridge toward the information booths, I remembered the fun times the four of us had at the Jersey Shore, where they'd played matchmaker for Joe and me. What if Terry didn't come back? Cresting the hill, Joe and I saw the mobbed tables and hundreds of people waiting to use the payphones. I didn't call my parents, as promised. I felt rebellious.

It was so crowded we could not make out anyone. We found a spot to watch the music, which provided a decent view when Richie Havens opened the festival with his rousing version of "Freedom." I was excited as I viewed the freaky crowds. At my religious college, I'd felt like a weirdo, but here were tons of kids like me with wild hair, dancing freeform, love beads flying. That night, it drizzled and then poured while we huddled together. We lit matches during Melanie's performance and laughed with Arlo Guthrie. Drenched, we retreated to the tent.

On Saturday morning, Joe and I slid down a muddy road, and we bumped directly into Terry and Leslie. We hugged and made plans to meet later.

Saturday afternoon, we all sat together, singing along to Country Joe's "Fixing to Die Rag." I could not imagine what was going through Terry's head as we sang along, "Be the first one on your block to have your boy come home in a box. One two, three, what are we fighting for? Don't ask me. I don't give a damn. Next stop is Viet Nam."

It was rainy and slippery, and we were soaked all the time, even in the tents. Our sleeping bags got soggy, and I didn't sleep much. But who wanted to rest while the super groups of rock were playing all night?

Everything was behind schedule with the show stopping when thunderstorms and torrential rains hit.

I drank red wine and bummed cigarettes, smoking more when I hung out with Joe. Nobody from our crowd had pot. Joe thought his brother was bringing half an ounce, but his brother thought Joe had it. At first, I was pissed. Then I realized it didn't matter. The crowd passed joints around during the music. We knew better than to take any of the acid.

Santana's jam on "Soul Sacrifice" was explosive. I was dancing and air-drumming along to the band's hot Latin percussionists as Carlos Santana's guitar riffs cut through the air. Joe bounced in his grassy seat, but I jumped into an impromptu conga line snaking around our section.

Around midnight, trying to stay awake, Joe and I got up and boogied to Credence Clearwater Revival. After their set, we retreated to our leaky tent, exhausted. We could still hear the music, so we hung out near the flap, drinking wine and listening. Janis Joplin whipped herself into a frenzy on "Piece of My Heart" and "Ball and Chain." I loved Janis and wanted to be watching, but we'd been out in the rain and mud for 12 hours.

I slipped on my last dry T-shirt and passed out. We were too tired to do more than kiss good night. The next morning, we crawled from the tent, dirty and thirsty, when the Jefferson Airplane jolted us to life, Grace Slick ripping into a fantastic set with "Somebody to Love" and "White Rabbit."

We left Sunday afternoon with no dry clothes left. I was wearing Joe's bell bottoms, rolled up. He had brought more outfits than I did. The concert was still going on. I wanted to stay longer, but he had to work Monday, and it was a long hike back to the car. I left the Woodstock Festival feeling incredibly high and elated.

We turned on the FM radio as we got closer to the city and heard that a million people had attended the festival. Something inside me shifted. I felt powerful. Together, Joe and I had been part of history.

Three years after Woodstock, Joe and I were walking through the woods when he told me he liked men and didn't want to keep stringing me along. He explained how he'd gotten out of the draft by telling a shrink he was gay. (I'd wondered about that.) He apologized for the deception and said he hoped we could be friends after I got over being mad at him.

I was upset about losing my boyfriend, but we remained close. A few years later, when I came out, having gay male pals made the transition easier. Joe escorted me to gay bars and was my queer wingman, hooking me up with my first lesbian lover.

I moved to the East Village, cut my hair short, and began freelancing. Joe got a crew cut and contact lenses. He lost weight and quit cigarettes. Moving to the Upper West Side, he worked as a trade magazine editor. I thought we'd hang out more, but he was involved with his Fire Island friends, and I lived downtown with my partner. We stayed close over the years. He lived for his summer house in the Pines and loved the rampant sex.

It's hard to conceive now how innocent we were at Woodstock. At the festival, we were terrified about our friends getting killed in an unpopular war in a foreign country—although Terry got a last-minute deferment. We had no idea what other kinds of dangers lay ahead: Twenty years later, right in our backyard, the AIDS epidemic wiped out a generation of gay men, including Joe. If the government had been more responsive to finding a cure for this plague in the early '80s, Joe and I might be attending Woodstock reunions together.

In August 1994, I went back to Yasgur's farm on the 25th anniversary of the Woodstock Festival. It wasn't the same without Joe. For many years, my former partner, Slim, and I had rented a rustic cottage in Sullivan County 20 minutes from the field. That Saturday, we took off for White Lake, where 50,000 people were camped (illegally) for the reunion, a far cry from the original 500,000. (It turned out the initial radio report we heard in '69 citing a million attendees, had been wrong.) This time, we parked close to the site. Local bands played on a rickety stage. Rumors flew that The Stones would show up. They didn't.

As we walked around, I remembered how Joe felt so connected to the scene that he thought he'd die at 27, like Janis, Jimi, and Jim. He was relieved when that birthday passed.

Visitors made little shrines with stones, crystals, flowers, love beads, photos, notes. I spotted an ACT-UP sticker. A local artist set up a huge piece of poster paper, urging those who attended the original festival to sign our names and record a message for those missing this reunion. I wrote:

Joe & Kate 69

Kate 94

Joe fought a two-year battle against AIDS, filing stories until the end and dying at 43 in 1989. When I visited him in the hospital, I made him laugh. At his funeral, a priest called him "Joseph." I wanted to scream, "His name is Joe!"

At the concert site, I imagined Joe coming down the path. I thought it might be fun to return, but it depressed me. I felt old. I felt queer. Everyone looked straight. I wondered how many others who attended the festival later came out like we did. It hit me that the Stonewall Riots and the Woodstock Festival occurred the same summer, 1969. Stonewall got less publicity, but now it seemed clear that the six days of fighting in Greenwich Village were more prescient and impactful than three days of peace and love.

In the summer of '69, I was a naive college kid who had my mind blown at the most memorable concert of my generation. Fifty years later, I still recall Joe when I hear The Who. He loved their lyric, "Hope I die before I get old." Tragically, he fulfilled that classic rock-and-roll wish.

Kate's yearbook photo, 1970

Acknowledgments and Credits

Major thanks to Naomi Rosenblatt, my publisher, who was excited when I pitched her my memoir in essays about living alone through the pandemic in New York City.

Thank you to my friend and colleague, Susan Shapiro, who runs the Thursday night workshop where I brought many pages of this book.

Thank you to all the writers who gave me feedback on this manuscript: Carol Binkowski, Nicole Bokat, Haig Chahinian, Brenda Copeland, Carol Crayton, Alice Feiring, Francisco Franklin, Lisa Lewis, Erica Manfred, Puloma Mukherjee, Tony Powell, Gabrielle Selz, Stephanie Siu, Candy Schulman, Jeff Vasishta.

Thank you to anyone who read pages whose name I may have omitted. Thank you to the writers of the Wednesday afternoon workshop for ongoing support. Thank you to Julie Dubow for computer assistance.

Major thank you to *The Village Sun* and publisher/editor Lincoln Anderson. At some point, as Lincoln continued to publish my pandemic essays, I realized I was writing a book.

The following fourteen pieces were first published in *The Village Sun*:
"Westbeth Feels Like a Ghost Town"
    (edited with additions)
"Stayin' Alive"
"The Kindness of Strangers"
"Melting Down in Lockdown"
"Gay Pride in Isolation"
"Will a Second Lockdown be Lonelier Than the First?"
    (retitled "Escaping to the Beach" with additions)
"Return From Trump Land"
"My Beloved Church Burns Down"
"Rita Houston: the DJ Who Saved My Life"
"The Pandemic Changed Me: I Learned to Like Clothes Shopping"
"Getting the Vaccine"
"The Second Time Around: Getting the Vaccine"

(The two vaccine pieces are rearranged in the book as "Scheduling the Vaccine on my Pandemic Birthday" and "Getting the Vaccine")
"Rooting for Hudson Street"
"My Life Needs a Reset Button"

Thank you to:

Disrupt Aging, who published "My Life Has Been Cancelled by Coronavirus." Ideas from that piece sparked my writing at the beginning of the pandemic.

Next Avenue, who published "Coming Out Again at 71" (edited with additions)

The Villager, who published "Saving the Memory of Old New York"

Medium.com, who published "Signing a Legacy"

Longreads, who published "Woodstock: My Queer Love Story"

Thank you to my family and friends for always being there. And especially to Jennifer Brougham for the weekly pep talks.

Thank you to my spiritual teachers whose Zoom classes got me through the pandemic:

Jennifer Gibson, yoga; Nadiya Nottingham, qi gong; Mary Ellen O'Brien, soul alignment.

Thank you to my incredible therapist, Dr. Ronnie C. Lesser.

Thank you to my neighbors at Westbeth Artists Housing, whose conversations kept me going during the pandemic.

Major shout out to the management and staff of Westbeth who assisted and protected residents during the pandemic. Their friendliness and dedication created a sense of normalcy during a crazy time.

CPSIA information can be obtained
at www.ICGtesting.com
Printed in the USA
FSHW020148031121
85892FS

9 781942 762812